Francis Wayland Parker, Lelia E. Patridge

Notes of Talks on Teaching

Francis Wayland Parker, Lelia E. Patridge

Notes of Talks on Teaching

ISBN/EAN: 9783337165772

Printed in Europe, USA, Canada, Australia, Japan

Cover: Foto ©ninafisch / pixelio.de

More available books at **www.hansebooks.com**

NOTES

OF

TALKS ON TEACHING,

GIVEN BY

FRANCIS W. PARKER,

AT THE

MARTHA'S VINEYARD SUMMER INSTITUTE,
JULY 17 TO AUGUST 19, 1882.

REPORTED BY

LELIA E. PATRIDGE.

THIRTEENTH EDITION.

NEW YORK AND CHICAGO:
E. L. KELLOGG & CO.
1891.

COPYRIGHT, 1883, BY

LELIA E. PATRIDGE.

CONTENTS.

                                                                          PAGE

INTRODUCTION: SKETCH OF COL. PARKER'S WORK..

TALK I.—PRELIMINARY........................ 19

    Attitude of the teacher toward the work—Foundation for true judgment—Price of success—The Quincy System;—what it is.—False and true motives of education—Definition of education—End and aim of the work—What the teacher must know—Study of principles indispensable.

    TECHNICAL SKILL............................ 23

    Vocal culture—Drill in Phonics—Training in reading and talking—Cultivation in Singing—Practice in Penmanship—Exercise in Drawing—Learning to Mould, in sand and clay—Gymnastic drill.

TALK II.—READING 26

    Importance of definitions — What is reading ? — How we get thought — Difference between hearing language, and reading — Definition of reading—Preparation made by child for reading—What he has to do to learn to read—The child's oral expression—Function of oral reading—The use of silent reading—Importance of correct habits of reading.

TALK III.—READING.—THE WORD 30

    How child acquires the spoken word—The law of association—The mental stimulus—Association of words with ideas—Objects

CONTENTS.

      PAGE

the best possible stimulus—The object method—The word as a whole. (Word method)—Devices to be used—Writing the word.

TALK IV.—READING.—SENTENCE.................. 35

Résumé of previous talk—Another means of association (the sentence) — The simplest step first (the word) — The sentence method—Child's natural expression to be retained.—Getting the thought before giving it—The method of imitation.

TALK V.—READING.—SCRIPT.................... 40

The written word—Script *versus* print—The change from script to print—Advantages of the script method—Reasons for use of the black-board—Why child changes readily from script to print.

TALK VI.—READING.—PHONICS................... 45

The spoken word; what it recalls—Explanation of slow pronunciation—Process of association between spoken and written word—Phonetic classification—Reconciliation of phonic and word methods—The law of like to like, and its uses—Details of the phonic method.

TALK VII.—READING.—APPLICATION OF PRINCIPLES 53

No new methods of teaching reading—Reconciliation of all, forms the true method—Importance of a careful selection of words—What words should be taught first—Directions regarding the first vocabulary—How to teach the first words—How to teach the first sentences—Devices for teaching the next step.

TALK VIII.—READING.—APPLICATION OF PRINCIPLES. (Continued)........................ 60

General directions for first lessons—Devices for teaching the first writing—Purpose of phonic analysis—First steps in slow pronunciation — Details of further training in phonics — The Sound Chart.

CONTENTS.

TALK IX.—Reading.—Application of Principles. (Concluded) 66

Directions for changing from script to print—First three years' course—Bad Habits; how caused—Devices for correcting them—General suggestions—Reading script work—The standard of excellence.

TALK X.—Spelling 71

What is spelling?—How is it learned?—Proper function of oral spelling—Purpose of spelling—First year's work—General directions.

TALK XI.—Writing 75

Reasons for teaching writing, early in the course—The forms of letters established—Correct training *versus* individuality—Everything should be carefully copied—Suggestions as to training in technic—Chart of letters, arranged in the order of teaching—Movement in writing; when it should begin—What is to be accomplished—Directions for training.

TALK XII.—Talking with the Pencil 80

How to treat child when it enters school—Exercises in talking with the tongue—Correction of bad habits, and inaccuracies—New idioms, and different parts of speech, taught objectively—What should precede talking with the pencil.

TALK XIII.—Talking with the Pencil. (Continued) 84

Thought before expression—First exercises in original written work—Suggestions as to training in capitalization, punctuation, etc.—The use of pictures—Object teaching; wrong, and right—Natural objects, as aids to language lessons—Descriptions, and stories—Important rules.

TALK XIV.—COMPOSITION.................. 89

Results of previous work—Every lesson a language lesson—Elementary and advanced Geography as an aid—History to furnish exercises in composition—Arithmetic will train in exact logic—How the study of Natural Science can be used—No necessity for the spelling-book—When should Grammar be taught?—Use of incorrect forms; false syntax, etc.—Parsing; word lessons; and diagrams.

TALK XV.—NUMBER.......................... 95

What is number?—Limitation of sense-grasp, and imagination—Objections to the object method—What can be done with numbers?—The fundamental four operations—What is the use of number?—How must number be taught?—First find out what the child knows—Facts the teacher should know—Calculation should be automatic.

TALK XVI.—NUMBER. (Continued)............. 103

Too much attempted the first year—Let child discover facts for himself—Teach the four operations at the same time—Reasons for this—Analysis and synthesis—A misunderstood point in Arithmetics—The learning of the language of number—Details of the step-by-step plan—When should the use of objects cease?—Advice to teachers.

TALK XVII.—ARITHMETIC..................... 110

When and how to begin teaching figures and signs—Details of succeeding steps to 20—Parker's Arithmetical Chart; 20 to 100—When can new numbers be taught without objects?—Nothing new in higher Arithmetic—Needless complexity of this study—Teach every new subject, objectively—How to bring about humility—Teachers need to study numbers of things—How much analysis?—Pupils should be led to discover thoughts for themselves—No explanations. We learn to do by doing—Education is the generation of power.

CONTENTS vii

PAGE

TALK XVIII.—Geography 120

Geography defined—Two parts of study: Structural Geography and History—First work; forming mental pictures of structure—The character of continental forms locates and fixes them in the mind—Illustration; the novelist and historian—All that is changing should be held in immovable forms—Vertical forms determine the character of continents—Also character of inhabitants, and history—Study of structure forms the basis of all Physical Sciences—Humboldt, Ritter, and Guyot and their work.

TALK XIX.—Geography. (Continued) 126

How can unseen forms be built in the mind?—Imagination and its laws—Importance of cultivating this faculty—Power of imagination in children—Directions for teaching the first steps in Geography—Work of the first five years in this study—Problems to excite curiosity, and lead to investigation—Reasons for teaching the continent before the county or state—The wholes of sense-grasp and of imagination—Mathematical Geography; when it should be taught.

TALK XX.—Geography. (Continued) 133

What is meant by building the continents—What a continent is—The Moulding in Geography. Its use and abuse—How to teach a continent by moulding—Map-Drawing. Its place and design—The order of teaching the continents—What follows this study of continental forms.

TALK XXI.—Geography. (Concluded) 138

The placing of continents in their relative positions—Lessons upon soil; vegetation; and animals—Mines and quarries located—The study of man; races; customs; habits, etc.—Governments and political divisions—Cities; industries; manufactures, and commerce—Latitude, longitude, and climate—What countries should be studied—Collateral reading—Illustrative collections of objects, and pictures—The great difficulty in the way.

TALK XXII.—HISTORY 143

What should be gained by study of History—Mental powers trained by this study—Use of fairy, and mythological stories—Details of indirect work from 4th to 7th year—How to take up the real study of History—Rules for selection of topics—Teach vital and interesting facts; not empty generalization—Fix events and scenes upon clear mental pictures of structure—Detailed directions for the teaching of a topic—Dates. What they should be—Caution, regarding the teaching of religious and political events.

TALK XXIII.—EXAMINATIONS 150

Examinations a great obstacle to good teaching—What is the aim of real teaching ?—What the object of examinations should be—The common standard false, and absurd—Illustration of the right mode of examining—Too much demanded of children—Examinations not the proper test for promotion—Freedom necessary for the teacher — The doctrine of responsibility—Give the good teachers a chance—Appeal for earnest, honest study and investigation.

TALK XXIV.—SCHOOL GOVERNMENT............. 156

The highest motive of school government—What is real attention ?—Two ways in which it may be gained—First try to make the subject attractive—Definition of natural teaching—Kindergarten principles all through education—Contrast between the two ideals in education—Teach everything with the stimulus of what the child loves—Illustration. Moulding, and Drawing—Demoralizing results of most primary teaching—Necessity of reward or punishment under the quantity ideal—Answer to the argument for stern discipline, etc.—The purpose of education—No time to spend upon made-up obstacles—Work best adapted to the child is best loved by him—The appeal to fear—Children study, and read the teacher—The question of Corporal punishment.

TALK XXV.—MORAL TRAINING.................. 166

End and aim of all education—What is character ?—Analysis into habits—Formation of habits—Everything done in school has

CONTENTS.

a moral or immoral tendency — Importance of training in self-control—Three causes that control the will—Child first controlled by mother or teacher—When child should exercise its own volition — Leading child to know, and do, the right—Habitual wrong-doing corrected by habitual right-doing—Necessity of knowing the child and its nature—Natural methods defined—Wrong methods immoral in their tendency — Natural methods enhance teacher's power for right—Attractiveness in subject arouses desire to attend—Doing through love of doing forms habit—Fear and force disgust and demoralize—Answer to argument in favor of old methods—Bad effects of the system of rewards, etc.—Truth should govern the will—Train child to seek, find, and use, the truth—Reason weakened through teaching generalizations—How the habit of seeking truth influences the after life—Training of skill without regard to thoughts—Effect when percision is the end and aim—Conceit, another outgrowth of the quantity ideal—The greatest barrier to true knowledge—Necessity for constant study on the part of the teacher—Careful selection of objects of thought presented— Basis of thought and imagination — Study of nature as a foundation for spiritual growth—Fill the mind with good, leaving no room for evil—Teacher, a constant object lesson to child — Tendency of children to read vicious literature—Its cause and cure—Plea for supplementary reading — Train children to love work — Natural love of child for expression in the concrete—Distinction between real work and drudgery—Importance of training in manual labor —Last words.

INTRODUCTION.

THERE is, perhaps, no name more widely known among the teachers of this country, than that of Col. Francis W. Parker. The results of his supervision of the Quincy schools have made him the most talked of, if not the most popular educator of our time. Whatever may be thought of him or his work—and it would be idle to deny that opinions differ regarding both — he is acknowledged, even by his opponents, to be one of those who are destined to mould public opinion. Concerning such the world is always curious. We desire to know their history, their environment, that we may judge their power.

Remembering this, I have thought that something of the man, as well as his methods, might prove interesting to the readers of the " Notes." I have, therefore, persuaded Col. Parker to give me the salient points of his life, more especially those that bear upon his career as a teacher, and these I have thrown into shape and order in the sketch which follows.

Francis Wayland Parker, born October 9th, 1837, in the town of Bedford (now Manchester), N. H., came of a race of scholars and teachers. His great-grandfather on his mother's side was Librarian of Harvard College, and a class-mate of Hancock. His mother taught for several years before her marriage, showing marked originality in her methods ; and all her children were born teachers.

From earliest childhood he thought and talked of being a teacher. It was always his dream, and his one ambition. His father dying when Francis was but six years old, at eight the boy was bound out, according to New England phrase, that is, apprenticed to a farmer till he was twenty-one. But nature was too strong for circumstance. A farmer he could not, would not be, and at the age of thirteen he broke his bonds, and started out into the world for himself. Without money, influence or friends, for he had angered his relatives by this move, he struggled on for the next four years, doing whatever he could find to do, and going to school whenever opportunity offered. Then he put his foot on the first round of the ladder ; he obtained his first school. It was at Corser Hill, Boscawen (now Webster), and he was paid fifteen dollars per month.

This venture proved successful, though many of his pupils were older than their teacher, and some (he says) knew more. The next winter he taught at Over-the-Brook in the town of Auburn, for seventeen dollars a month, and "boarded around." From this time his services were in such demand in the town, that he taught, not only the winter schools for the next three years, but opened a "select school" on his own account during the autumn months. One term of teaching in Hinsdale, and one in the grammar school of his native village, ended his work in New England for several years.

In the fall of 1859 he received a call to the Principalship of the graded school at Carrollton, Ill., and there he remained till the breaking out of the war in the spring of 1861. Finding, then, that loyalty to the Union was the one qualification in a school-master for which they had no use in that vicinity, he resigned his position before his committee had fully decided that they wished for it, and was immediately offered a better one with a higher salary at Alton, Ill. This he declined and started for the East, where he at once enrolled as a private in the Fourth New Hampshire Regiment just forming. He fought all through the war, became lieutenant, captain, lieutenant-colonel, and brevet-colonel. He was wounded in the throat and chin at the battle of Deep Bottom, August 16th, 1864, was taken prisoner by the confederates at Magnolia, N. C., and released just as peace was declared. Then with the remnant of his regiment he returned to New Hampshire, and was mustered out of service August, 1865.

At the call of his country he had left the school-room; now she required his services in the field no longer. Where next? Many ways were open to his choice. Military preferment, political office, excellent business positions were offered to him at this time. but he declined them all. His passion for teaching was too strong for these to tempt him. He never wavered for a moment, not even when his best worldly interests seemed to be at stake. A teacher he was born, a teacher he would live and die. He accepted the Principalship of the North Grammar School of Manchester, N. H., at a salary of eleven hundred dollars, and held the position for three years. From there he went to Dayton, Ohio, in 1869, to take charge of the school in District No. 1. Here he had the supervision not only of the grammar grades, but of the primary; and now his primary work began. He had all along had his own way of doing things, and had from the very first his conception of how teaching should be done. Indeed, he tells with some amusement at his own audacity, that when only eight years old, he rose in school one day and informed the teacher that he didn't know how to teach! Even war, with all its horrors, did not wholly absorb his mind from its favorite theme. Often, as he sat before the camp fire, or lay in his tent at night, he studied how the mind grows, and planned many of the methods which have since made him famous. It was in Manchester where he used to work all day, and then spend half the night preparing for the next, that he first began to apply his theories. But in the primary schools of Dayton, he felt for the first time that he had begun at the beginning of the great work of mind development. At the end of the year he became Principal of the Dayton Normal School, a position he held for two years, being then elected Assistant Superintendent of the City Schools.

No one who steps out of the beaten track can walk long in his new path unchallenged. To desert the old, to fail in respect for the traditional, to imply that customary ways of doing things might not be the best ways, is treason, and high treason. This Col. Parker was made to feel, and feel keenly. Though a soldier, he loved peace better than war, but he began to see, as time went on, that his fighting days were not yet over. More and more he found himself antagonizing the convictions of his fellow-teachers, as day by day he grew away from the time-honored traditions of his vocation. They would not agree to his views, he could not agree to theirs; and one party must be in the wrong—which was it? Where did truth lie? It would seem with the majority. But he would not give up what seemed to him so clearly right without reasons. He would consult the highest authorities in the art of teaching, and learn if he were wrong. Accordingly, in the fall of 1872, he went to Germany, and entered King William's University, at Berlin, for a two years' course in philosophy, history, and pedagogics.

It need not be said that his opinions found confirmation strong in that centre of intellectual development; and he returned to his native land eager for an opportunity to put his theories, now fully fledged, into practice. When it comes to pass in this world that the right man finds the right place, we have a way of saying, "How very providential!" as if affairs were only occasionally under the care of Providence. But it was certainly a singularly happy coincidence that just about this time one of the most intelligent school committees of these United States, located at Quincy, Mass., made a discovery which forced them to a conclusion, and that in turn decided them to make an experiment. Their discovery was, that after eight years of attendance in the public schools, "the children could neither write with facility nor read fluently; nor could they speak or spell their own language very perfectly." Their conclusion was, "that the whole existing system was wrong—a system from which the life had gone out. The school year had become one long period of diffusion and cram, and smatter had become the order of the day."

[It is not to be understood by this that the Quincy schools were any worse than the average, but merely that they had a committee intelligent enough to comprehend their true condition.]

Acting on this conclusion, they had decided to try to remedy matters. But they were busy men, not specialists in education, and wise enough to know that they were unequal to this difficult and delicate work. Thus they had come to the decision to find some one to do it for them. They would try the experiment of having a Superintendent of Schools. That committee found the man they sought, in Francis W. Parker. So Col. Parker went to Quincy, and nothing since the time of Horace Mann has created such a sensation as his five years' supervision of those schools.

Said his committee in their report after he had left them, " For five years the town had the benefit of his faithful, intelligent and enthusiastic services. In these years he transformed our public schools. He found them machines, he left them living organisms ; drill gave way to growth, and the weary prison became a pleasure house. His dominant intelligence as a master, and his pervasive magnetism as a man, informed his school-work. He breathed life, growth and happiness into our school-rooms. The results are plain to be seen before the eyes of every one, solid, substantial, unmistakable. They cannot be gainsaid, or successfully questioned." Said Charles Francis Adams, Jr., in his paper on the " New Departure in the Common Schools of Quincy," " The revolution was all-pervading. Nothing escaped its influence ; it began with the alphabet, and extended into the latest effort of the grammar-school course. So daring an experiment as this can, however, be tested in but one way—by its practical results, as proven by the experience of a number of years, and testified to by parents and teachers. Out of five hundred grammar-school children, taken promiscuously from all the schools, no less than four hundred showed results which were either excellent or satisfactory, while its advantages are questioned by none, least of all by teachers and parents. . . . The quality of the instruction given has been immeasurably improved."

Such a success as this, heralded abroad by the thousands who visited the Quincy schools, could not fail to bring advancement in its train. Accordingly, when in 1880 Boston gave the country Superintendent a call to "come up higher," and be one of its Supervisors, he accepted, and at the expiration of his time of service (two years) was re-elected for a second term. In October, 1882, Col. Parker received an urgent call to the Principalship of the Cook County Normal School (just outside Chicago), at a salary of five thousand dollars; and later, the same year, was offered the Superintendency of the city of Philadelphia, at a still higher salary. In December he resigned his position in Boston, and yielding to his overmastering desire to teach, declined the office of Superintendent, which Philadelphia would gladly have given him, and accepted instead the charge of the Normal School in Illinois. The first day of January, 1883, he entered upon his duties as Principal of the Cook County Normal School, where he is now working with all his characteristic force and spirit.

With greater opportunities than have ever been granted to him before, with an experience broadened and deepened by the failures and successes of the past, with his old-time energy and enthusiasm no whit abated, we have faith to believe that the future will show results, which shall make what he has done in the past seem but the crudest of beginnings.

THE MARTHA'S VINEYARD LECTURES.

The first of the year, 1881, Col. Parker received an urgent request from the Directors of the Martha's Vineyard Summer Institute that he should become the head of the Department of Didactics, at their next session, beginning in July of the same year. Although working already to his utmost, it was a great temptation to have a few weeks of his favorite pursuit thus offered him in the midst of so much supervisory work. Consequently, he decided to give three weeks of his much needed summer rest for this purpose. The matter being decided hastily, and at the last moment, was not properly advertised, and the Class in Didactics that first year was small to what it would otherwise have been, numbering only fifty members.

The following year, feeling that here was an opportunity for wide-spread influence, and much good to be done, he returned to the Vineyard. He found that his small beginning of the summer before had been a true beginning, for not only did many of the class of '81 return, but they showed that they had been making a study of the great art of teaching, and came back better prepared for the lectures, by their year's experience and observation. This season the Class in Didactics numbered nearly one hundred and fifty members, representing twenty-three States and Nova Scotia. Of this number there were forty-seven Principals or Heads of Departments, seven Superintendents, eleven Kindergartners, and two Institute Lecturers. The course extended through five weeks, and the following were the Lecturers and Teachers:

PRINCIPAL, COL. FRANCIS W. PARKER,
"Art of Teaching."

DR. WILLIAM T. HARRIS,
"History and Science of Education."

DR. LARKIN DUNTON, *Head Master of the Boston Normal School.*
"Principles of Teaching."

PROF. MOSES TRUE BROWN, *Professor of Oratory in Tuft's College.*
"Reading in Grammar and High Schools."

PROF. H. E. HOLT, *Supervisor of Music in Public Schools, Boston.*
"Teaching Music to Little Children."

PROF. HERMANN B. BOISEN, *Author of Boisen's New German Course.*
"Principles of Teaching Modern Languages."

H. P. WARREN, *Principal of the N. H. State Normal School.*
"Teaching History."

PROF. L. ALONZO BUTTERFIELD, *Teacher of Elocution at the Newton Theological Institution, and Associate Principal with Alex. Graham Bell, in School of Vocal Physiology, Boston, Mass.*
"Phonics."

INTRODUCTION.

Miss Ruth R. Burritt, *Principal Kindergarten Training School, Phila.*
"How to Teach Form by Moulding Clay."

Miss Hetta Clement, *First Assistant, Coddington School, Quincy.*
"Moulding Geographical Forms."

Mrs. Mary D. Hicks, *Late Supervisor of Drawing, Syracuse, N. Y.*
"Lessons on Drawing."

Mrs. M. Frank Stuart, *Boston School of Oratory.*
"The Delsarte Method—Its Uses and Abuses."

Miss Lelia E. Patridge, *Instructor at Teachers' Institutes, Penn.*
"Gymnastic Drill."

Col. Parker, yielding to the strongly expressed desire of his pupils and fellow-teachers, has consented to resume his work at the Institute the coming season; but it will be his last year at the Vineyard. His regular work in the West is too arduous and absorbing to permit of any outside interests. Besides, he cannot afford to fall before the fight is ended; and not even his splendid vitality could long endure the strain of such exhausting and continuous labor. However much we of the East may regret the loss of his inspiring lessons on the great art of teaching, we must be willing to forego them after this season, not only for his own sake—that his days may be long, but for the sake of the little children of the land; for when he dies they lose their warmest friend, ablest champion, and wisest benefactor.

Philadelphia, March, 1883.   L. E. P.

I HAVE carefully examined the MS. of the "NOTES OF TALKS ON TEACHING" prepared by Miss Patridge, and find it substantially correct

FRANCIS W. PARKER.

CHICAGO. ILL.. April 19, 1883.

NOTES OF TALKS ON TEACHING.

TALK I.

PRELIMINARY.

I SHALL try in these lessons to help you learn more of the great art of teaching. We have come from widely different sections, and are, for the most part, strangers to each other, and may find it a little difficult at first to draw together. But a common interest will unite us in the bonds of sympathy and good-fellowship We have all seen teachers who were so self-satisfied that they seemed—to their own minds—to have rounded the circle of teaching, made the circuit of knowledge and skill complete, and closed their minds against the entrance of all further impressions. Such can never learn till the barriers of conceit behind which they have intrenched themselves are broken down. There are others, the opposite of those just described, who stand like empty pitchers waiting to be filled; they accept any and all methods which are popular, or have some show of authority. Such teachers are imitators merely, and will change when any novelty is brought to their notice. No one was ever great by imitation; imitative power never leads up to creative power. Just here let me say that I shall object quite as strongly to your taking the methods which I may present, unquestioned, as I should to your acceptance of others in which I do not believe.

Again, there are teachers who have some good ways, but who are so prejudiced that they have no regard for anything outside their own work ; they cling to the old, have a ready-made objection to the new, and have ceased to examine. Facts are the eyes through which we see laws. There is no better founded pedagogical rule than that the facts must be known before generalizations can be. It follows, then, logically, first, that we cannot know which is the better of two methods without knowing both ; second, that we cannot know which is the best without knowing all ; and, third, that we cannot know any method without knowing the principles which the method applies. Finally, no one can fairly judge a method by seeing it in operation once or twice, because the application may not be correct, and that cannot be judged unless the foundation principles are known.

The great difficulty in the way is, that teachers are not willing to pay the price of genuine success—that is, untiring study in the most economical directions—hard labor. The demand for good teaching was never so great as now, and no matter where you are, if your work is good it will attract attention.

I have been often asked to explain the so-called Quincy system. So far as I have been able to understand this system, it does not consist of methods with certain fixed details, but rather presents the art of teaching as the greatest art in all the world ; and because it is the greatest art, demands two things : first, an honest, earnest investigation of the truth as found in the learning mind and the subjects taught; and, second, the courageous application of the truth when found. In the talks which follow, the only real substantial help I can give you is to aid you in such investigation. All the truths that you may learn must be discovered by yourselves. In this way alone truth is made a living power. Nothing is farther from my present purpose than to have you take what I shall say without the most careful scrutiny. The great mass of teachers simply follow tradition, without questioning whether it be right or wrong, and it requires very little mental action to glide in the ruts of old ways.

The work of the next hundred years will be to break away from traditional forms and come back to natural methods.

Every act has a motive, and it is the motive which colors, directs, forms the action. Consequently, if we would understand the educational work of to-day, we must know its motive, bearing in mind the fact that due allowance must be made for the stupefying effects of long-established usage. The motive commonly held up is the acquisition of a certain degree of skill and an amount of knowledge. The quantity of skill and knowledge is generally fixed by courses of study and the conventional examinations. This is a mistake. In contrast with this false motive of education, to wit, the gaining of skill and knowledge, I place what I firmly believe to be the true motive of all education, which is the harmonious development of the human being, body, mind, and soul. This truth has come to us gradually and in fragments from the great teachers and thinkers of the past. It was two hundred years ago that Comenius said, "Let things that have to be done be learned by doing them." Following this, but broader and deeper in its significance, came Pestalozzi's declaration, "Education is the generation of power." Last of all, summing up the wisdom of those who had preceded him, and embodying it in one grand principle, Froebel announced the true end and aim of all our work—the harmonious growth of the whole being. This is the central point. Every act, thought, plan, method, and question should lead to this. Knowledge and skill are simply the means and not the end, and these are to work toward the symmetrical upbuilding of the whole being. Another name for this symmetrical upbuilding is character, which should be the end and aim of all education. There are two factors in this process : first, the inborn, inherited powers of the mind, and, second, the environment of the mind, which embraces, so far as the teacher is concerned, the subjects taught. The subjects taught, then, are the means of mental development. To aid in the mind's development the teacher must know, first, the means of mental and moral growth, which are found in the subjects taught ; and, second, the mental laws by which alone these means can be applied. Knowing the mind and the means, he can work toward the end, which is growth. Method is the adaptation of means of growth to mind to be developed, and natural method is the *exact* adaptation of means of growth to mind to be developed. To acquire a knowledge of the mind and of the means by which the mind may be developed is the study of a lifetime. Let us stand with humility before immensity.

In the beginning, then, the study of methods aside from principles is of little use ; therefore, that investigation should lead to a knowledge of principles is all-important. There are two lines of investigation : the direct one is the study of mental laws, or the investigation of the facts out of which the generalization of principles is made. The second, and indirect way, is the study of the application of methods in detail, in order to discover through such details the principles from which they spring. Let no teacher rest satisfied with a study of the mere details of methods, but use them as illustrating and leading back to principles.

TECHNICAL SKILL.

In order to train children how to do, we must be able to do ourselves ; hence the great importance of that preparation on the part of a teacher which will result in skill in the technics of school work. First of all, the voice should be trained, for a clear musical voice is one of the teacher's most potent qualifications for success, and cannot be overrated. Drill in phonics is necessary, not only to gain the ability to give the slow pronunciation with ease and with natural inflections, but as an aid to perfect articulation and pronunciation. That every teacher should be an expressive reader is self-evident, but it might not occur to all that to be an eloquent talker is also one of the requisites demanded by the New Methods. Faults of tone, modulation, and manner are propagated by the teacher, as well as false syntax and incorrect pronunciation. Then, too, every teacher should be able to sing, and sing well. Music fills the air with beauty, and in the school-room everything should be quiet and musical, with never a harsh note. Failing in this the school lacks harmony. Writing is the second great means of language expression, and should follow immediately upon talking. A teacher who cannot write well, cannot teach writing well; for the copy on the blackboard should be well nigh perfect. Skill is the expression of power, and drawing is the second best way of expressing thought. Given the skill to draw, and a teacher is never helpless, for then he can teach, even if everything else is taken away. Besides, I see a future in drawing which I see in nothing else in the way of developing the mental powers; hence the demands made upon teachers for knowledge and skill in this art must increase with every year. Moulding in sand is one of the best possible ways to teach geography, and should precede map drawing. Moulding in clay is a valuable means of form teaching, and is also the best of preparations for drawing. Last of all, gymnastics—the training of the whole body—is of the utmost importance, not only to insure symmetrical physical development, but to aid in the establishment of good order. Mental action, as you know, depends largely upon physical conditions, and therefore we should train the body that the mind may act. Believing that the skill of the teacher in these directions measures in a great degree his power to do good work, I have endeavored in this course of lessons to provide you with the best of teachers for these different departments. Now, a word of caution : time and strength are both limited, therefore don't try too much ; but that you may become experts in these technical matters, let me add, whatever you do try, be sure to follow it up.

TALK II.

READING.

In the teaching of any subject it is of great importance that we have a clear definition of what we teach. Not a definition in words alone, but a definition in thought that comprehends what we teach in the most definite manner. The question before us is, What is reading? The answer to this question that I shall give, is, Reading is getting thought by means of written or printed words arranged in sentences. Thought may be defined as ideas in relation. Ideas are either sense products, or derivations from sense products. We get thought, first, by seeing objects in their relations; second, by thinking of things in their relations without their presence; third, by seeing pictures or drawings of objects in their relations; and fourth, by language. We get thought by language in two ways. First, by the spoken language, and, second, by the written or printed language. To illustrate, I put this hat upon the table. Here you see the relation of two objects, and you think *The hat is on the table.* I draw or sketch the hat on the table, and it brings to your mind the thought *The hat is on the table.* I say, "The hat is on the table," and you think the same. I write on the board the sentence, *The hat is on the table*, and that conveys to your mind the same ideas in their relations. Thus we get the same thought in four ways; the only difference in the result is, that the thought gained from seeing objects in their relations is generally clearer.

Hearing language is getting thought by means of spoken words arranged in sentences. Reading, as I have said, is getting thought by means of written or printed words arranged in sentences. It would be well for us to examine these two operations, hearing language, and reading, in order to see in what they are alike, and in what they differ. The arrangement of words in sentences, that is the idioms, are precisely alike. The thought in the mind, gained either from hearing language or reading, is identical. The only difference lies, then in the fact, that in one case the word is spoken, and in the other it is written or printed. I am sure you have said, as I have given my definition, that reading is the oral expression of thought. That is oral reading. But you will see at once that we may get thought—and by far the greater part of reading is confined to this process—and not give it to others by means of the voice. If we comprehend oral reading in our definition, we should say that reading is the getting and giving of thought by means of words arranged in sentences.

Not less in importance to the definition of reading, is the thorough knowledge of the preparation a child has made for learning to read, how he has made it, and exactly what is to be done in learning to read. This may be briefly stated thus : First, a child has acquired ideas from the external world by means of his senses

Second, he knows the ideas in their relations, that is, he has thoughts. Third, the child has associated spoken words with these ideas. Fourth, he has associated idioms or forms of sentences with his thoughts. Fifth, he has learned to utter these words and idioms in order to express his thoughts. This is a brief summary of the process of learning to talk. How he has done this will be discussed in another place. Exactly what the child has to do in order to learn to read may be clearly stated thus : The ideas that he has associated with spoken words are to be associated with written or printed words. If I am not mistaken, this is the sum and substance of learning to read.

Oral reading may be further defined as the vocal expression of thought that is gained by written or printed words. A child has already learned to express thought orally, by means of five or six years' continual practice. The emphasis, inflection, and melody of most children's voices can rarely be improved. The child should be trained in no new way, then, of expressing thought in oral reading. Unfortunately the beauty and strength of what the child has already gained is entirely ignored, and a new and very painful process of oral expression is initiated. What is the use of oral reading? Talking enables us to see the thought in the child's mind ; oral reading, to the teacher has no other use. Oral reading, then, enables the teacher to know whether the thought is in the child's mind in its fulness, strength and intensity. If, however, the long preparation of the child in talking is overlooked, and a new and stumbling process of slowly pronouncing words is begun, the indispensable function of oral reading is entirely destroyed. The thought may or may not be in the child's mind, his half-groaning utterances never reveal the fact.

What is the use of reading? We return to our definition: reading is getting thought by means of written or printed words arranged in sentences. Comprehensively stated, reading opens to the mind all the learning and erudition of the past. To the teacher, however, it is of the utmost importance, for reading is thinking, and thinking is the mind's mode of action ; and all mental development is rightly directed toward action. Study of text books, then, if it differ from reading, the difference may be found simply and solely in intensity. In study the thought gained may be clearer and more complete than in mere reading. You can judge for yourselves then, fellow teachers, of what immense importance it is for the little child to form correct habits of reading ; and you know by experience how easily incorrect habits may be cultivated, habits that will dishearten a child in his attempts to read, and make words, instead of being clear mediums of getting thought, actual barriers to the truth they were intended to convey.

TALK III.

READING.—THE WORD.

The child at five years of age has acquired ideas in their relations, has associated spoken words with these ideas, and idioms with the thoughts or related ideas. The process of learning to read, then, must consist of learning to use the written and printed word precisely as he has used the spoken words. Learning to read is learning a vocabulary of written and printed words, so that the child may get thought through the eye as he has done through the ear. It is a matter of great interest to the teacher of little ones to know just how the child acquires the spoken words. The process is a very simple one; an object is presented and the word spoken. That is, the idea produced by the object and the spoken word are associated in one act of the mind, which we call an act of association. We all know that only by means of a mysterious mental law, called the law of association, are we enabled to recollect anything. Words are used under this law to recall ideas. The word recalls an idea after a certain number of repetitions of these acts of association. In the same way related ideas are associated with idioms or sentence forms.

Every act of the mind is affected by some stimulus or

mental excitement coming either from without or within the mind. As a rule, the greater the stimulus the more effective the act. The little child, for instance, sees an elephant for the first time. The sight of the huge, strange beast stimulates the mental action of the child to an unwonted degree. The perpetual question of the little one, "What is that?" comes to his lips with great fervor. The answer, "The elephant, my child," will be likely to remain in its mind forever. The spoken word, then, is acquired by repeated acts of association. The number of these acts necessary depends in a great degree upon the stimulus of each act. For instance, the greater the stimulus the less the number of acts of association required, and *vice versa*. What we have said of words may also be applied to the learning of idioms.

Now, the question is, in learning the new means of recalling ideas by means of the written words, should there be the slightest change in the general method? A word is used simply and solely to recall an idea. It has no other use. It can be learned only by association with the idea recalled; and the sole question for the teacher is, to know how best to associate words with ideas. I think we can lay down this one rule as fundamental: in all the teaching and the study of the art of teaching, little children to read, that that which aids directly in acts of association of words with their appropriate ideas, aids the child in learning to read, and any other method, detail of method or device that does not aid the mind in these acts, hinders the child in learning to read. To this one rule, then, all our discussion of the art of teaching reading must return. Everything must be reconciled with this or it is wrong.

The first question, then, is, What is the best way of bringing about the acts of association with the best possible stimulus? It is plain common-sense to continue the method that has developed a fixed and powerful habit of learning new words, namely, the presentation of objects as the highest and best stimulus to acts of association. This is strikingly true in teaching the first few words. The written or printed word is a new, strange object. It repels rather than attracts. No stimulus, then, can be found in the strange hieroglyphics that look more mysterious to the child than Hebrew or Sanscrit do to us. Tide the child over his first difficulties by using the active energy of a fixed habit. Simply repeat that which has been repeated thousands of times, present the object (a favorite one of the child's), and say the word, not with the lips but with the chalk. The child's consciousness is filled with interest for the object, leaving just room enough for the new form to find a resting-place. On the other hand, try to fill the child's mind with the word itself, and you fill his soul with disgust.

The spoken word has been learned as a whole. It is more complex, and therefore more difficult to learn than the written word. Every spoken word is learned as a whole, and we have no reason to believe that the child has the slightest consciousness that the spoken word has any elementary parts. The attempt to teach him the elementary parts of a spoken word, while he is learning to talk, would prove disastrous. Why, then, should not the written word be learned as a whole? Why introduce a new process, when the old one has been so effectual? Indeed, there is no doubt that any attempt to separate the written word into parts, or to combine the parts of a word into a whole, directly and effectually hinders the acts of association, and therefore obstructs the action of the child's mind in learning to read. The tendency of unscientific teaching has set steadily and strongly for the last thirty years toward woful and useless complications in details of instruction. The return to real teaching is signalized by a strong leaning toward simplicity. The height of the art of teaching, as in all other lesser arts, is found in simplicity. Hold up the object and write the name. Say just enough to lead to the proper mental action and no more. The fewer words the better. Begin with objects. Select those objects most interesting to the child.

Next to objects I shall place sketches upon the blackboard, done in the presence of the child, so they may be associated with the names of the things drawn, and the sentences that express the relations of the objects. Third, pictures may be used effectively. Fourth, conversations of the teacher that will bring the ideas to be associated with words vividly into the child's consciousness. Fifth, stories may be told with the same result. How long should objects be used? Until the child will actively associate new words with ideas without the presence of the objects or pictures of the objects that produced the ideas. No teacher who watches the faces of her little ones will fail to note when this time has fully come.

If the principles that I have here given are true, then you will have a basis of truth for the discussion of the art of teaching little children to read. This method, to use a popular but not a correct term, may be called the associative or objective method. Learning the word as a whole, without trying to fix the child's attention upon its parts before it becomes a clear object in the mind, is called the "word method."

The question, no doubt, will arise in your minds, if the old alphabet method is entirely laid aside and the phonic method is not used at the outset for the analysis of words: How is the form of the word fixed in the mind? The answer is a simple one: The best way to fix any form in the mind is to draw it.

TALK IV.

READING.—THE SENTENCE.

I will repeat the fundamental principle of the art of teaching reading. Learning to read is learning a vocabulary of written and printed words. Each word is learned by repeated acts of association of the idea and the word. That which helps in these acts of association, and that alone, should be used in teaching reading. All other means are hindrances. I have shown that the effectiveness of the acts of association depends on the stimulus or excitement to the act. This stimulus comes primarily and mainly from the side of the idea. The vividness of the idea or mental picture in the consciousness, with the appropriate word, determines the result. The greatest difficulty to be found in the process of learning to read is in learning the first few words. The habit, so strong in the mind, of learning the spoken word, is to be carried over and used as a power in learning the written word. The word itself should be subordinate and secondary in interest to the child, to the idea that excites the mind. The word is to be learned consciously as a whole, and any attempt to analyze or synthesize it hinders the act of association by absorbing the attention. The means used to arouse the mind to acts of association, I have told you, are, objects, drawings upon the blackboard, made under the eye of the pupil, pictures, conversations, and stories. But there is another and still stronger means of association after the first few words have been learned, and that is the arrangement of words that recalls ideas in their relations or thought. Every object that we recall or think of is recalled in space. The more interesting the relation of the ideas one to another, the stronger will be the association. That is, it is a great help in learning words to learn them in sentences. We do not learn the word in order to read the sentence, but we read the sentence in order to learn the word. The question may here be asked, Why not begin with the sentence, as many do, with great success? My answer is, that the first written words, as I have said, present the greatest difficulties to the child. We can hardly comprehend how mysterious the strange forms are to the little one. We may get an inkling of the trouble if we have ever begun Greek, Hebrew, or Sanscrit. We may recall the fear that came over us, when we looked forward to the time when we must use the meaningless forms to get thought. The successful learning of the first few words, it seems to me, depends upon presenting the simplest obstacle to be overcome, and in making the child, the little learner, as unconscious as possible of the difficulty. The simplest step, then, consists in following a fixed and powerful habit of the child, by presenting a favorite object, and saying with the chalk just what the tongue has so often repeated. I have no doubt but what the skilful teacher could successfully begin with a whole sentence. My point is, that it is much simpler and easier to begin with the single words. Just as soon, however, as a few words have been learned, for instance, fifteen or twenty, short sentences should be taught by the objective plan ; so that when the child sees the sentence he is able to get the thought that it expresses. There are many words that mean nothing alone, which should always be taught in phrases or sentences.

We come now to the discussion of oral reading, or getting thought by means of written or printed words arranged in sentences. A thought is ideas in their relations, and may be called the unit of mental action. A sentence, therefore, is the unit of expression. We cannot learn a single word without recalling the idea it expresses in some relation. You will remember what I have said concerning the different ways of getting thought. First, directly through the senses, by seeing, hearing, etc., objects in their relations. Second, by pictures and drawings. Third, by language, both oral and written. In all these cases the thought is the same in the mind, differing only in degrees of intensity. The written sentence is simply one way of getting thought. The child has already, by long and continued practice, learned to talk, and to talk well. One thing above all others I wish to impress upon your minds, here and now—do not teach him to talk in any other way—that is, when he gets the thought by means of the written sentence, let him say it as he always has. Changing the beautiful power of expression, full of melody, harmony, and correct emphasis and inflection, to the slow, painful, almost agonizing pronunciation that we have heard so many times in the school-room, is a terrible sin that we should never be guilty of. There is indeed not the slightest need of changing a good habit to a miserable one, if we would follow the rule that the child has naturally followed all his life. *Never allow a child to give a thought until he gets it.* Remember, and keep on remembering, my dear teachers, that the child has learned to talk, and that that teaching which mangles this grand power is needless and worse than useless. Let the child get the thought himself, in the easiest possible way, by means of the written sentences. One of the worst ways of teaching reading may be called, for want of a better term, the method of imitation. Now you will see that the valuable act of the mind, the thing to be done, is the child's getting the thought for himself and by himself by the means, I repeat, of written words. If the teacher reads the sentence to the child, the child gets the thought through the ear from the teacher's lips, and the one thing he ought to do is prevented. I do not wish to be understood that the teacher should not read to the child. The teacher should make herself the best possible model of good reading, and through her reading present a high ideal of expression for the child to attain. What I wish to impress upon you is, the one pedagogical principle that stands above all others—we learn to do by doing. Oral reading has one function, one use to the teacher ; it is a means of knowing, as I have said in a former talk, whether the thought is in the mind of the reader, how it is there, if every relation is known, and the intensity of the thought felt by the reader. This grand function of oral reading may be perverted or entirely destroyed. First and foremost, by not waiting for the child to get the whole thought before he gives it. Second, by training the child to imitate the teacher's voice, her pauses, emphasis and inflection ; and, third, by a useless struggle with the parts of the word in forcing analysis before the whole word is clearly in the mind. The alphabet method is the best possible means of obstructing the mental action of the child in learning to read ; too early phonic analysis the next. With the child thought has always controlled expression. Why should we throw this grand power aside, and try to teach a child oral expression by means of pauses and imitated inflection and emphasis ? The initial capital of a sentence and the punctuation have one use—they enable the child to get the thought. When the thought is in the mind they have no use. You will see, then, that if you follow the principle—thought controls expression—much of the labor and toil of the teacher, in trying to force artificial expression by training a child to pause at commas and periods, to raise the voice or let it fall at the end of sentences, to give stress when they see diacritical marks, is not only useless, but positively injurious and nonsensical.

TALK V.

READING.—SCRIPT.

THE written word to the little child has no element of attraction. It is, on the other hand, a repelling object. I have tried to show how the difficulties of learning the first words may be overcome by the stimulus of the idea in acts of association. It is a matter of great importance to steadily overcome the repulsion occasioned by the written word. This repulsion will grow less and less, and the acts of association will be made easier by continued familiarity with the new forms, if the interest and the appetite of the child for words is sedulously cultivated, through the pleasure that the objects and pictures excite. All words are made, as you know, of only twenty-six different forms. The less the mental action it requires to see these forms, the easier will be the acts of association. It is important to impress these forms upon the mind in an easy, natural, semi-unconscious way. As I have shown, the best possible way to impress the word forms upon the mind, is to write them—to make them. We hear the objection very often that a child does not learn the letters by the new method. He does not learn their names, but he learns *them* by continually making them. What is the best proof that any object is clearly in the mind? A word description is weak beside the representation of the object in drawing. This brings us to the question so often mooted, whether we should use print at the beginning, or print and script, or script alone. I will try and present the arguments in favor of using script alone, not denying, however, that script and print may be used at the same time with good effect. When two or more ways of teaching are presented, all of which may be defended by good reasons, reasons that do not directly violate a principle, the question of choice then becomes a question of economy. If we begin with print, it certainly fixes the printed forms in the mind by reproducing them on the slates, so that if the teacher uses print alone at the beginning, she should train the children to make the printed forms. But, making the printed forms is not a means of expression that a child ever uses after the first few months, or the first year. Writing is the second great means of language expression. It should be put into the power of the child just as soon as possible, in order that he may express his thoughts as freely with the pencil as with the tongue. This fact needs no argument. Written expression is as great a help to mental development as oral expression; and, indeed, in many respects, it stands higher. Written expression is silent, the child must give his own thought, in his own way; thus developing individuality. The greatest difficulty in all teaching in our graded schools is the sinking of the individual in the mass. In written expression we find a means of reaching individuality through the mass. Why not, then, begin at the beginning with this mode of expression that the child must use all his life, and every day of his life?

Why not teach printing and script together? Because it violates the rule of perfect simplicity. Train the child to use one set of forms, made in one way, and one alone. In my experience, extending over eleven years of supervision of primary schools, I have never known the failure of a single class to change from script to print, easily and readily, in one or two days. What, then, is the use of print at first? What logical reason can be given for its use, if the step from script to print is so very simple? The writing of the words by the child on blackboard, slates and paper, furnishes a vast amount of very interesting and profitable busy work. In writing the first word the child begins spelling in the only true way. In writing the first sentence the child makes the capitals and punctuation marks, and if he is never allowed to make a form incorrectly, it will be almost impossible for him ever to write a sentence incorrectly—that is beginning it with a small letter, or not using the proper punctuation at the end. In writing the words, the child follows exactly the method of learning the spoken language. Spelling is the precise corelative of pronunciation. The child hears the spoken word and strives to reproduce it by his voice. The child sees the written word, and reproduces it with his pencil. He gets the thought by means of the written word, and gives it back just as he gets it—he is talking with his pencil. He is ready to tell you any time, orally, what he is writing.

In the first three years' work, talking with the pencil

may be used as a greater means of learning to read than all the books of supplementary reading. When the child writes the first word, the unity of all language teaching is begun. Getting thought and giving thought by spoken and written words should be united at the start, and grow through all future development as from one root.

What advantages has the blackboard and crayon over the chart and printed book in elementary reading? First, the words are created by the hand of the teacher before the eyes of the children, as the spoken word is created. Second, the word is written alone in large letters, separated from all other objects of interest except the object it names. How different the confused mass of black specks upon the printed page. Third, the attention of the little group is thus directed to one object in a very simple manner. Fourth, words are learned by *repeated* acts of association. The great fault with charts and primers is that they do not repeat words times enough for the child to learn them. On the blackboard, on the other hand, these repetitions can be easily made. It is of great importance that the first one hundred words should be learned thoroughly. Superficial work is always bad work. From the first, then, the child should write every word he learns from the blackboard, and just as soon as he is able to write sentences the word should invariably be written in sentences.

The child should be trained to read from his slate all that he writes. The reason why the change is made so easily from script to print used to puzzle me. I only knew that it could be done, but could not tell the reason why. Script and print are very nearly allied in form. The first print was a crude reproduction of old manuscript. Both, indeed, have changed since the art of printing was discovered, but the resemblance remains. The child, as you know, has a wonderful power of seeing resemblances. Like comes to like in his mind because his mental pictures are not filled out with that which produces the differences. This, to my mind, is sufficient reason for the surprising ease with which the child changes from script to print.

TALK VI.

READING.—PHONICS.

I propose to speak to-day of the use of the spoken word in assisting acts of association between the idea and the written word. It is very often urged that the spoken word is sufficient to recall its appropriate idea, and thereby bring about an act of association between it and the written word. That, as the ideas are already in the mind of the child, the spoken word alone is needed to recall them. Those who hold to this doctrine fail to understand the great economy of mental action that is brought about by the stimulus of the object. Were I to teach you a foreign language, German, for instance, how much quicker and easier you would learn the words if I were to present the objects and speak or write their names. This is thoroughly understood to-day by the best teachers of modern languages. If we adults can learn a foreign language so much easier by the object method, it can be readily inferred how necessary the use of objects is to the little child. When the old habit of learning spoken words is carried over into the learning of written words, that is, after a hundred or more words have been learned, probably the spoken word will then be sufficient to bring about the required acts of association. When a child does not need the stimulus of objects, pictures, etc., then their use should cease. Any good teacher will not fail to observe when this time comes to the child. The spoken word, then, aids in recalling the idea, and at the same time names the written word. The spoken word is associated with the written word, so that it recalls the written, and the written recalls the spoken. Deaf mutes learn the written words without the intermediate help of spoken words, and it is found that with the use of objects these unfortunate beings learn written words with as much, if not greater, rapidity than the children who have perfect hearing. Notwithstanding this fact, the spoken word has a use in learning to read, but it may be badly misused. For instance, when it is associated with the written word alone, and the written word is not associated with the idea. In this case, the reading is not the getting of thought, and, therefore, not real reading, but simply mechanical word pronouncing without the slightest inspiration from the thought. There are methods of teaching reading, whose sole aim is to train children to pronounce words with little or no regard to the thought. To the casual observer the results seem surprising. To the real teacher they are the sounding of empty words. The use of the spoken word, then, in teaching reading, must be to assist in acts of association. To use them for any other purpose is a hindrance in learning to read. The question, then, is, How can spoken words be used to help associative acts? The spoken words have been acquired by the child before he enters school. He knows how to make every sound in the language, and to combine them in pronouncing all the words he knows. He has learned the spoken words as wholes, and is not conscious of the elementary parts of a word, although he can combine them without the slightest hesitation. The spoken word consists of the articulation of one elementary sound or a succession of elementary sounds. An elementary sound, with the exception of the sound of *h*, requires for its articulation a certain fixed position of the vocal organs. Change the position of the vocal organs, no matter how slightly, and the sound must change. Between a few combinations of two sounds the articulation continues, producing peculiar modifications of sound brought about by various positions of the vocal organs that they must take in changing from the position required by one sound to that of another. If, however, these glides were made between each and all of any combinations of the sounds of the language, the intermediate sounds would be innumerable. As it is, forty sounds are all that are given in making the spoken words of the English language. In changing, then, from the position of the vocal organs required to make one sound, to that of another, there must be, except in glides, an actual suspension of sound. In pronouncing ordinarily, these pauses between sounds are too short to be perceptible to the ear. Make these pauses perceptible, and we do, what I think is wrongly termed, spell by sound. As phonic analysis has nothing whatever to do with spelling, is oftentimes a hindrance rather than a help to English spelling, I prefer to call the act of articulating each sound with a perceptible suspension of the voice between two sounds—slow pronunciation, following the German term—*langsamer ausprache*. Now, it should be borne in mind, that in reality the spoken words alone are pronounced slowly, the written words cannot be. It is a mistake to say that certain letters have several sounds, several sounds are represented by one letter. The process by which a word is made to recall a spoken word, or a letter is made to recall a sound, is exactly the same as that by which the written word recalls the idea—viz., the process of association. When the first word is learned, the spoken word is associated with the written word. The spoken word and written word are learned as wholes. I have tried to show that the written word is fixed in the mind by writing it. That when one word, for instance, *rat* is taught and written, the word *cat* can be more easily seen and more easily copied; for the word *cat* contains two thirds of the forms of the previous word. In this way we see that as the different forms are impressed upon the mind, the repulsion of the word, or the difficulty in grasping it is overcome, and successive associations made easy. In the same way the spoken word may be associated with the written words, so that the written words will recall the spoken with greater ease. As the written words become more clear in the mind, the separate parts of the written word may be associated with the separate articulate sounds, so that the difficulties in the acts of association may become less and less; that is, new words may be pronounced and known at sight. The great danger is, that children may be trained to the skilful pronunciation of words without knowing them. A word is only known when it recalls its appropriate idea.

There are two great obstacles in the way of the successful teaching of the so-called phonic analysis. One is more apparent than real, and that is, the fact that different sounds are represented by the same letter in the English language. In a purely phonetic language (which, by the way, does not exist), each sound is represented invariably by one character. If the English language were phonetic, it would greatly lighten the burden of learning to read and write. But a careful examination of the words learned by a child will show that the difficulties are not so great as they are often represented to be. If we begin, for instance, with the short sounds, a child may learn at least two hundred words that are purely phonetic to him. I have calculated and classified the words in thirty-nine pages of the New Franklin Primer, in the whole of Monroe's Charts, and in the first forty pages of my Supplementary Reader, First Book. There are 456 words in all: 205 of which are purely phonetic, 216 are words whose pronunciation is indicated by their form; and only the 35 remaining may be called entirely unphonetic. After a child learns this number of words he has formed a fixed habit of learning new words, and all active use of primary methods may cease. What, then, is the use of burdening the child with mangled and twisted print or diacritical marks? Phonics may be used as a great help in teaching primary reading, if the natural growth of the child's power is carefully followed.

The second difficulty in teaching phonics is found in the apparent opposition of the word and phonic method. The word must be learned as a whole, and any early attempt at word analysis simply retards the teaching. The struggle to analyze a new word, or to build it up from parts, as I have already explained, absorbs the attention and prevents the act of association. These two methods, that seem to be in direct opposition to each other, may be entirely reconciled by closely following well-known mental laws. The child, as I have said, knows how to make all the sounds in the language in their word combinations. He is not conscious of a single separate element. Obviously, the first step to be taken is, to bring these elements slowly to his consciousness. This may be done by training the child to pronounce words slowly (spell by sound). I have found by repeated experiments that the little child will understand me when I pronounce words slowly in a natural manner, nearly as well as when I pronounce in the ordinary way. The child may be trained by imitation to pronounce slowly with great readiness and skill. This should be carefully done before any direct association is made between articulate sounds and the word that represents them.

One of the greatest activities of the mind is the coming together of like to like. It may be called the law of analogies. It begins, as all good things do, in perfect unconsciousness on the part of the child. When a child says, "I seed," for I saw, and "I goed," for I went, the child is unconsciously following this law of analogies. The same law is in operation when the child spells all words phonetically, without regard to the absurdities of English spelling. Using phonics, in teaching reading, in the proper way, simply intensifies this law. If the word method were used, pure and simple, the child's unconscious mental activity would seek out and use the analogies of the language, in associating new written words with the same sounds he has learned to associate with them. When we teach words in phonic order, as, for example, rat, fat, cat, mat, sat, pat, this law of like coming to like in the mind is made more effective. But when at the proper time the articulate sounds are consciously associated with the letters that represent them, we use this mental activity in the most economical way. Great care, however, should be taken not to force the growth of this mental action so as to conflict with the other and more important law of learning words as wholes. These whole words cannot be analyzed until they are clear mental objects. The process, then, of using phonics may be given thus : First, train the child to recognize words when pronounced slowly. This may be easily done, if the teacher pronounces slowly in easy, natural tones. The greatest obstacle that I have found in phonics is the inability of teachers to do this. Second, train the child to pronounce slowly by imitating the teacher's voice. All this should be done, as I have said, before any direct association of articulate sounds is made with written words. Third, after a few words are taught, let the teacher in writing words give each articulate sound as she makes the character that represents it. Do not require the children to imitate the teacher until they do so of their own accord. Fourth, have the children begin to pronounce slowly, without even a suggestion from the teacher, the words which she writes. Phonics may be thereafter used with great effect in teaching reading. Thus, you will observe, that by this process the spoken word retains its unity as long as it is necessary, and the way is carefully prepared for the conscious analysis of words when the proper time comes. This will be indicated by the child's own spontaneous action.

All new words, then, that come within the child's acquired analogies of sound may be readily associated with their appropriate idea with little or no aid from the teacher. Give the child the power to help himself as soon as possible, and at the same time please remember not to violate any known laws of his mental growth.

TALK VII.

READING.—APPLICATION OF PRINCIPLES.

In this discussion of the art of teaching reading, I have tried to explain the principles that underlie the so-called object, word, sentence, script and phonic methods. Each of these methods has been discovered by teachers in the past, and generally each has been applied by different teachers as the only true method. Probably the exact date of the discovery of each method cannot be given, but the youngest of these, the script method, is nearly one hundred years old; and the oldest, the phonic, is described by Valentine Ickelsamer, a contemporary of Luther's, in a book written in 1534. No one would claim the title of inventor of a new method, if they had studied the history of the art of teaching reading. Each one of these methods was discovered in the action of some mental law. So far as they go, and used in their own proper place and proportion, they are all natural methods. The difficulty is in using one method to the exclusion of all others. It is like using one power of the mind and leaving four others inactive. The fact is, that the object, word, sentence, script, and phonic methods form one true method in teaching reading. Each should be used in its own time, place and proportion, in such a manner as to arouse and strengthen five faculties of the mind instead of one. This reconciliation of most methods that have been discovered in the past, is true not only of teaching reading, but everything else. We might say that everything now done in the school-room, in the way of teaching, is right, in its place; but the trouble is that things get frightfully misplaced. Precision, for instance, may take the place, and crush the evolution of thought, and thought growth may override precision. It seems to me, that the great duty of the teachers of this age is, first, to know all the great things that have been discovered by the teachers and thinkers of the past, and to reconcile them into a science of teaching. I shall now endeavor to apply in practice what I have given you in theory; in which I trust you will see that all the methods I have given can and should be used as one.

The preparatory exercises that should always precede the teaching of primary reading, I will give when I discuss the teaching of language. We will suppose that the child has had these preparatory exercises, and is ready to be taught reading. The first question to be settled is, What words shall be taught? (Learning to read, you will remember, is learning a vocabulary of written and printed words.) The first general answer to this question is, The oral words the child has already gained. The idea must always be acquired before the word can be. All through the education of the child this rule should be carefully followed. Education may be said to consist, first, of enlarging the range of ideas; second, in relating these ideas in various ways.

The value of a word depends wholly upon the

value of the idea it recalls. It is of great importance to select carefully the vocabulary to be taught the child during the first year; and it is of greater importance that the selected vocabulary should be slowly and thoroughly taught. That is, that repetitions of the word should entirely suffice to put the word within the automatic use of the child.

Much time and very good teaching is wasted by not following the step-by-step rule, by which everything done is thoroughly done. It is far more important to teach 20 words well than to try to teach 200 imperfectly. The first vocabulary selected should contain about 200 words, to be taught in script on the blackboard. In selecting this list of words three things should be taken into account. First, the *favorite* words of the child. Those words which would naturally arouse most interest in the child should be taught first. Second, the words should be arranged in phonic order —generally the short sounds are taken first. With these words, all the unphonetic words, like *where*, *there*, etc., that serve to introduce the idioms used by the little child. Teaching words in the phonic order, that is, the order of vowel sounds, serves, as I have previously explained, to intensify the law of analogies on which the phonic method is founded. I may say here, that the phonic order should not be followed at the expense of the interest of the child. Every word and sentence should bring up a bright and interesting picture. One should not hesitate to introduce any new word for this purpose. The first words taught should be names of common objects. Now it is true that the objects most common to the child have names in which only short vowel sounds occur, such as *fan, cap, hat, cat, mat, rat, bat, bag, rag, flag, hen, egg, nest, bell, fish, dish, pig, rabbit, ship, dog, doll, top, fox, box, cup, tub, mug, jug, nut.* The second thing to be observed in selecting the list is, the words used in the first book or books that the child will read.

No First Reader extant furnishes repetition enough for the thorough learning of the words. It is better to select the vocabulary from the first parts of three or four different readers. If this is done when the child begins the print (after 150 or 200 words have been taught in script), he can read with great ease and delight 150 or 200 pages in print. We will suppose, then, that the vocabulary has been carefully selected; that the preparatory oral work has been done; that the teacher has selected fifteen or twenty objects, or models of objects, to aid in teaching the first few words. The pupils have been carefully divided off in groups of five or six, according to their mental strength. The work would naturally begin with their brightest group. (Never tell them that they are bright, however.) The teacher is at the board, surrounded by a little group of children, who have been made to feel quite at home in the school-room, and who are ready and eager for any new step, because everything they have done in the school-room has given them pleasure. They have unbounded faith in the power of the teacher to lead them into green pastures filled with the most delightful shrubs and flowers. The teacher holds up an object as she has often done before; but now, instead of giving its name orally, she says, "Hear the chalk talk," and slowly writes the word. Let me say here, that the articles *a*, *an*, and *the*, should always be written with the words, and the article and word should be pronounced as one word. Write the name of the object several times. Let the teacher point to the word, having put the object down, and say to the child, "Bring me a —" pointing at the same time to the word. Let the teacher hold up the object and ask, "What does the chalk say this is?" having the pupil point to the word. These exercises should not occupy more than five minutes. The next lesson shows a new object, and write its name as before. Let the child take the two objects, one in each hand. Let the teacher write the name, and ask him to hold up the objects, first one, and then the other, as the names are written. This plan may be safely followed till ten or fifteen words are taught. In review of words, all the names may be written; let the teacher point to the different names and have the pupils bring the objects; then the teacher holds up the objects, and lets the pupils point to the names; and last, have the pupils point and give the names without the objects.

The first sentence may now be taught. Let the child take, for instance, a fan in his hand, and be led to say "This is a fan." The teacher writes the sentence on the board, and says, "The chalk has said what you said, what did the chalk say?" The child, holding the fan, says, "This is a fan." Write in place of *fan* successively, all the words that have been taught. Have pupils take the objects and read the sentences. Change *this* to *that*; place the objects at a little distance from the pupils, and repeat all the sentences as before. Change *that* to *here*, and repeat all the sentences, having the child hold the appropriate object as he reads each sentence. Change *here* to *there*, and repeat as before. Change the singulars to plurals, and change the sentences accordingly, using *these* and *those*, *here* and *there*. Write questions beginning with *where*, as, " Where is the fan ?" and let pupils answer orally by holding up the object, as " Here is the fan." Put the objects on the table, and ask the question by writing it on the board—" Where is the fan ?" After this answer, write the answers and have pupils read them. When a dozen sentences have been written, have the pupils read the whole successively. Introduce new words as before with objects. Qualities of objects may be brought in next ; as " The red box ;" " The white fan ;" " The fat rat ;" and reviews made by the schedule just given—*this, that, these, those*, etc. Place objects in different positions, as the fan in the hat, the cap in the box, and write sentences, describing them. Little exclamatory sentences may here be introduced with good effect, as " Oh, what a pretty fan !" " See the little doll !" " Oh, there is the cat !" " The cat is sitting up !" " Isn't she funny ?" Directions might be written on the board which the pupil reads silently, and complies with ; such as " Come to me." " Sit down." " Stand up." " Shake hands." " Run." " Jump." " Skip." " Hop." " Laugh." " Cry," etc.

The next step may be the writing of little connected stories on the blackboard. A very good way to write stories, or sentences connected in thought, is for the teacher to sketch a picture on the board. Let her make a plan for a picture containing quite a number of objects. Let her sketch one object before the little group, talk, and then write sentences about it, and arouse curiosity as to what the picture is to be. Thus, one picture may serve for several lessons. A large wall picture may be used in the same way. In all object lessons, lessons on plants, animals, and color, the words and sentences should be written upon the board.

TALK VIII.

READING.—APPLICATION OF PRINCIPLES, CONTINUED.

Some general directions to be followed in teaching these first lessons may be of service. I will give them here.

1. Carefully introduce each word which of itself recalls an idea, by first presenting the object, sketch or representation of the object, or by bringing the picture of it vividly to the child's mind by means of conversation or questioning.

2. All words that do not recall ideas except in their relations, should be taught in phrases or sentences.

3. Try to make every thought and its expression real to the child, and when it can be done, suit the action to the word.

4. Be sure the child has got the thought before you allow him to make an attempt to give it.

5. Have the child get the thought by means of the written words, and not by hearing the sentence read.

6. Do not teach emphasis, inflection and pauses by imitation. Thought will control expression. If the thought is in the child's mind in its fullest intensity, the expression will be appropriate.

7. Train children to read in pleasant, conversational tones. free from harshness, monotony, or artificiality.

8. Never allow the children to read carelessly, or to guess at the words.

9. To arouse a desire for new words, and a love for the reading lesson, observe the following rules :

1. Teach the words very slowly at first.

2. Put the words taught into many different sentences.

3. Write short sentences, and then make very slight changes in them—generally of a single word—in order that the children may be successful every time they try to read a sentence.

4. Wait patiently until they grasp the thought, and if they are dull be very patient.

5. Have always a bright picture behind each word or sentence, which the child shall see vividly with his mind's eye.

The children should be trained to write on their slates the first words they learned from the blackboard. Several devices may be used for this. First, the children, following the teacher, may write the word in the air. Second, they may trace the word. Third, they may write the word line by line as the teacher writes it. (The teacher, by the way, should be an excellent penman.) Fourth, the children may write the word without any help from the teacher, copying it from a large and well-nigh perfect copy on the blackboard. The slates should be ruled. The same word may be copied several times. No matter how badly the child writes the first word, praise him if he has tried, and do not discourage him if he has not tried. Imbue him with your own faith that he can do it. When the sentence is written, have him write the sentences in the order I have given for the teaching of sentences. Be sure that he always begins the sentence with a capital, and uses the correct punctuation mark at the end of the sentence. Have the pupils read everything they write. Use short sentences at first. Never allow a child to read a sentence till he has the thought in his mind, and never allow him to express the thought in any other way than by talking. If he does not talk well train him to do so, orally, by object lessons. Introduce all new idioms in the same way. Repeat the words until you are sure they are thoroughly known.

The use of the phonic method may begin the first day the child comes to school, with the phonic analysis of the spoken word, which I prefer to call slow pronunciation. The purpose of this exercise is to bring distinctly to the child's consciousness the separate sounds of which the spoken word consists, and to give him such practice as will enable him to utter all the elementary sounds of the language purely and easily. But no attempt should be made at this time to associate these elementary sounds with the letters that stand for them. That comes later. The child should first become accustomed to *hear* the separate sounds and to *utter* them; and the exercises for this purpose should be among the first given to the child, and be carried on side by side with the oral language work from day to day. I will describe in detail the first steps of this work. When a few exercises in the repetition of sentences have been given, the teacher may, without changing her tone of voice, pronounce slowly (spell by sound) one of the words in a given sentence. For instance, the teacher, pointing at the clock, says, "There is a c-l-o-ck." The pupils will repeat the sentence as before, without hesitation. Or the teacher may say to the children, "Touch what I name: n-o-s-e, m-ou-th, f-a-ce, d-e-s-k," and the pupils will perform the acts promptly *if the teacher does not change her tone.* Then pronounce single words slowly, and ask pupils to tell what you say. Pronounce whole sentences slowly, and ask the pupils to repeat them in the ordinary way. Direct pupils to "s-t-a-n-d u-p; s-i-t d-ow-n, etc. As soon as they have become accustomed to hearing the slow pronunciation say single words slowly and let them imitate. (One sound may be given at a time, the pupils repeating—as, "m," "*m*," "ou," "*ou*," "th," "*th*.") It is not well to let the pupils pronounce a word slowly and immediately pronounce it in the ordinary way, as in a spelling exercise, because they should have the feeling that when they have once uttered the sounds, they have pronounced the word. After this, pronounce words in the ordinary way, and ask the pupils to pronounce the same words slowly. Let pupils pronounce slowly any words that they may think of. Those children who have defects in articulation should have special drill. To assist them in uttering the sounds correctly, the right position of the vocal organs should be shown. Words mispronounced should be corrected by imitating the teacher, and by repetition until the correct habit is formed. The preliminary exercises, both in oral language and in phonics, should be carefully graded, beginning with those which are very simple. There should be frequent reviews, and the exercises should be short—five minutes at first, and never at any time more than ten minutes. Practice on the sound chart is of great service. Begin by articulating each sound separately, and asking the pupils to imitate you. Each sound may be repeated once or twice or three times, both slowly and in quick succession, the pupils imitating. In this exercise the sounds may be given in the order indicated in the chart which is given below, but this chart should not be written on the board at first, not until it is needed for the purpose of associating the sounds with the letters in teaching reading.

SOUND CHART.

CONSONANTS.

m	n	ng	l	r
p	t	ch	k	c
b	d	j	g	
f	th	s	sh	
v	th	z	zh	
h	wh	w	y	

Vowels.

SHORT SOUNDS,

a   *e*   *i*   *o*   *u*   *u* (as in pull)

NAME SOUNDS,

a   *e*   *i*   *o*   *u*

LONG SOUNDS,

a   *au*   *oo*   *oi*   *ou*

TALK IX.

READING.—APPLICATION OF PRINCIPLES, CONCLUDED.

WHEN 150 words or more have been taught, write a nice lesson on the blackboard in script, and have the pupils read it; then, after the day's session, erase the script and print the same lesson in the same place. Call up the pupils the next morning, and have them read the lesson. Do this two or three times, and the pupils are ready for the chart or a book. It is better to take the chart first. In my experience of several years in changing many classes from script to print, this simple process has sufficed. One rule should be strictly followed. Never point out or allude in any way to the difficulty in learning print. You should have, besides a good chart like Monroe's or Appleton's, at least five or six sets of First Readers. They are very cheap, and you can induce your committee to buy them, providing you do good work. Read one book until the sentences become difficult, and then take another. (Never let the children point to words with their fingers, and train them from the first to find their places for themselves.) Two years at least should be spent with the average child in learning to read First Reader reading, and the third year may be profitably spent in commanding Second Reader reading. There is immense economy in going very slowly. If the primary work is thoroughly done, there will be little or no need of teaching reading as reading after the fourth year.

BAD HABITS.

I am quite sure that many of you have asked the question, to yourselves at least, while I have been explaining the principles and methods of teaching primary reading as I understand them, What shall we do with children whose teaching has been all wrong from the beginning? Who have been taught by the alphabet, phonic, phonetic, or word methods without the life-giving principle of the thought? Who struggle with each particular word in a painful way, and drawl out the sentences as if there were no beautiful pictures behind them? Who have been led through a dreary waste of empty words in a harsh, unnatural manner? What shall we do with these children? you ask. It is a very difficult question to answer, for two or three weeks' wrong teaching will leave their scars in the child's mind forever; crippling every action, and obstructing every step. The elocutionists, by scores, reap a rich harvest from the bad teaching in primary schools. The trouble with the voices generally is, that the natural, easy, pleasant tones of the child are changed to harsh, unnatural utterance. Something may be done indeed for these unfortunate victims. First, I would say, no matter what grade the children may be in, put them into the easiest possible reading, even if you have to begin with the First Reader. Select the most interesting and the most dramatic pieces. Dialogues, brisk, sharp dialogues are very good. Drop oral reading for a time, and lead the children to see vividly the picture that lies behind the words. Have them tell you in their own language what they see in the word-pictures. When they are very much interested, and are talking with great freedom, ask one to read a short sentence. The pupils will feel the shock (if the teaching be skilfully done) from cheerful, interesting conversational tones, to dull, prosy word-pronouncing. Thus you can slowly lead them to form new ideals in reading. Your whole mind as a teacher should be concentrated on the one great thing of leading your pupils to get the thought, or seeing mentally the picture. If you hold steadily to this one purpose, you may be able to lead them to read naturally. It is a good plan to question them sharply upon the sentences they are reading. Take a paragraph like this, for instance : " Five little peas in a pod ; they were green and the pod was green, so they thought all the world was green, and that was as it should be." And then question, thus : " Where were the peas ?" " How many peas were there ?" " What kind of peas were they ?" " What color were the peas ?" " What color was the pod ?" " Because they were green, what did they think ?" The pupils can answer correctly, only by the closest attention to the thought expressed by the paragraph. Ask them occasionally to read a whole sentence. In this way children may be led out of the wilderness. Remember, also, to give pupils a great deal of interesting reading adapted to their vocabulary and thought.

SUGGESTIONS.

Two kinds of reading exercises, at least, should be given to the pupils. First, exercises in which every new word is carefully taught upon the blackboard, before the lesson in the book is read. Second, tests in which pupils try to read new selections without preparation. These tests should be frequently given—once a week at least. The same general rules should be observed in teaching reading in books. Do not let the child read a sentence aloud until he knows its words and its meaning. If the sentence is long he should be allowed to express the thought by phrases or clauses. As a rule, do not let the pupils in a class know who will be called upon to read next. Do not give the thought to the pupils orally, but let them get it for themselves. Do not require them to read the same lesson over and over again, lest they lose their interest in it. It is a good plan to have the pupils close their books and tell in their own words what they have read. In the second year, when composition has been well begun, require pupils to write one thing they remember of what they have read; then two things; three things; and finally let them write the whole story as they remember it. Ask them to read orally the sentences, descriptions, and stories they write. A large number of sentences, plainly written on slips of paper, or cardboard, may be successfully used. Give each pupil a slip. If one pupil reads a sentence correctly, give him another slip to read. For busy work, give pupils slips to copy, and let them read what they have copied. Let pupils take a number of slips and arrange them for busy work, into a little story. Then let them read the story from the slips, or read it after copying it upon their slates. Single words, written or printed upon cardboard, may be put together into sentences and read. When the teacher finds, by false emphasis or wrong inflection, that the thought has not been correctly apprehended by the reader, questions may be used with good effect. By this means the attention of the pupils will be turned directly upon the thought, and their answers will be given with natural tones and expression, as in talking. Gradually they may be led to utter the whole sentence with expression.

Reading and composition should be taught together, the one assisting the other at every step. Let pupils read what they write from a copy, from dictation, and in composition. If pupils are trained, as they may be, to express thought correctly and easily in writing, their compositions may be made as profitable as supplementary books in teaching reading. Let pupils read one another's compositions. In testing the script work, the list of words taught may be rapidly written in sentences and short stories. If the pupils can readily read these, the teacher may feel confident that the words have been well taught. In book-reading the tests should be from books that pupils have never read. Before reading a paragraph aloud, a short time should be given the class to read it silently. Finally the standard of excellence is indicated by these two questions. First, has the reader correctly apprehended the thought? Second, has he used correct pronunciation, distinct articulation, and natural tones?

TALK X.

SPELLING.

READING and spelling should come first in the child's school-life, so as to finish them, and get them out of the way. If the preparation is thorough, and the teacher skilful, not a great amount of time need be given to either. To continue the teaching of spelling, as is usually done, through all the years of a common-school course is a wasteful expenditure of time and strength. What is spelling? Spelling is making the forms of words correctly, it is writing correctly, and should include capitals and punctuation. Oral spelling is not spelling *per se*, it is a description of the word. Spelling is the co-relative of pronunciation. I hear a word pronounced over and over till I can give it back. I see a word spelled over and over till I can give it back. The only difference is, that spelling is the written or printed form, and pronunciation is the spoken. We learn to do a thing by doing it ; by doing it repeatedly ; by doing it right every time ; by doing it until it is well done. It follows, then, that we learn to make a word by making it ; to make it accurately by making it accurately ; to make it easily by making it many times. In order to know how a word looks we must *see* it, and the best means of seeing a form is to draw it ; therefore drawing (or copying) words is the best means of receiving distinct mental impressions of written words. If I spell a word orally, the names of the letters recall their forms and you combine them in your imagination. It is just as absurd to try to learn drawing by oral description, as it is to try to learn how to spell a word from hearing it spelled orally. The proper function of oral spelling is to describe word forms already in the mind ; not to bring them into the mind by acts of imagination. The most natural and economical way of learning to spell, is to write words until we can write them automatically.

What is the purpose of spelling ? During the first year it is entirely to prepare for composition or "talking with the pencil." Indeed, all spelling is for the sake of composition, and it has no other purpose. The words first taught on the blackboard in reading, and the commonly used and constantly recurring words of the child, in short, the script vocabulary, should be the words first spelled. Bear in mind the fact that word forms sink into the mind very slowly, and that patient waiting and working are especially required just here. Make every step with the small child a success, otherwise you may disgust the mind with its failures. You must wait for idea growth, which cannot be forced. Therefore do not have a child reproduce words without a copy during the first year. Spend this time in preparation for talking with the pencil. Training in talking with the tongue is one of the best ways of preparing for this work. If this be properly done, the words will drop off the pencil as easily and naturally as they drop off the tongue. Faith has a great deal to do with results. It is a great element in successful teaching, as well as humility. Accept crudities. The best thing which the child can do is always excellent. You may take the hand and help the child, or allow him to trace the form, but I like best to let him work out his own salvation. Get to sentences as soon as possible, and after that keep to sentences, for they are the written forms of thought expression, and the stimulus of the thought enables the child to recall the word-forms in writing, just as it does in reading. Do all this work easily and slowly, and in the doing of it let the child alone and don't fuss with him. If a child makes anything wrong, rub it right out, make it a sort of dissolving view. Have him acquire the power of copying from the blackboard with *perfect accuracy* any sentence he can read. Never accept any careless work. Don't scold, but let the work vanish under the sponge with quiet celerity, and have the child do it over. A better vocabulary can be gained by writing than by reading. Form, during the first year, a nucleus vocabulary of written words, so distinctly fixed in the mind that they can be reproduced instantly, without copy and with perfect accuracy. Train children to know when they can see a word mentally, and when they cannot. In other words, have them know when they don't know. Say to them, "Don't write that word if you don't know it," but never allow them to guess. Every guess brings before the children a wrong form, and as only one is right the wrong are in a majority. I would never allow a child either to see or to hear any wrong forms. When they get into the High School they may come in. There will be plenty of time for false syntax then. When a word is spelled wrong, don't explain, say nothing, except perhaps, "You didn't see right," and erase it at once. Cultivate constantly the child's desire to do work well, and that desire will absorb all his energies, leaving no time for idleness or mischief. In dictating, read the sentence in your best voice, and *read it but once.* Pupils should be trained to hear perfectly, as well as to read expressively. When they can write readily and accurately from dictation, begin to train them to talk with the pencil. As soon as this is accomplished, all spelling *per se* may cease, and this branch of study be taught in composition. They should be able from this time forward to write page after page without a mistake in spelling, and with capitals and punctuation marks correctly placed,

TALK XI.

WRITING.

I HAVE called your attention to the fact that the second great means of expression, *i.e.* by writing, should be placed in the power of the child just as soon as possible after he enters school. One great advantage of written, over oral, work, is that the written enables the teacher to get at and develop the individuality of the child. In oral lessons, the answers of bright children are constantly copied and imitated by others. Whereas, in written composition each child must express his thoughts for himself and by himself. By means of the command of writing, the child can be trained to do a great deal of busy work, thus keeping his mind and hand constantly employed. The third reason for teaching writing very early in the course is, that the work necessary to the command of good legible handwriting may be entirely finished ; and the time heretofore taken throughout the eight or nine years for writing, may be used for something more profitable. Writing may be kept in the best condition throughout the whole course, if language is properly taught, and the rule, "never allow any careless work," closely followed.

There are two things to be acquired in writing: First, the forms of letters. Second, movement with the pen. The conventional forms of the letters has been established by the highest authorities in writing in this country. All the systems in our schools have substantially the same forms. The slant of letters (between 51 and 52 degrees) is very nearly identical in all. It is not my purpose to discuss whether these forms are right or wrong. It is true that when pupils enter the upper primary and grammar grades, they are trained to make these established forms. It is a great saving of time and toil to make these forms right in the beginning, so they will never have to be changed. Allow children to display what is called their individuality at the start (that is to write any way and every way), and it is much more difficult to train them into good handwriting when they take the pen, than it would be if they had never written at all; many claim that fixed forms of writing injure the child's individuality, or destroys the character displayed in writing. As well might we say that the child should be allowed to pronounce words as he pleased, as the fixed pronunciation acquired by imitation of correct standards would seriously affect his individuality. The most potent reason why teachers do not train children to write correctly is, that they cannot write well themselves, and will not take the trouble to learn. Teachers should train themselves by constant and careful practice to write with a great degree of perfection on the blackboard, so as to give the children a good ideal toward which they can work. In this question of character in writing, there is one rule that teachers would do well to follow ; in writing as in all other things, — precision precedes ease. That is, let the established form be thoroughly acquired, and then, when the child has formed a character, that character will go into the writing. The painful attention now required to decipher the manuscript of most great men and women could be given to something else more beneficial.

The foundation of spelling should be learned entirely by writing. As we have shown in the application of the principles of teaching reading, every word that the child learns from the blackboard should be carefully copied on the slate or paper. These copies, as I have said, should be written with exceeding care. At the same time technical writing should begin. In this there are certain elementary principles that are the key-notes of the whole. Find them and follow them, and you are certain of success. Begin with one letter and stay upon that letter till it is learned. The child must have the ideal to follow, and that comes slowly into the mind through the eye. Begin with this fundamental form, found in the first letter taught, and work on until you get it, even if it takes a year or two years. The children will not tire till the teacher gets tired. Have the standard, the ideal clear, and they will work toward it patiently. Get them to master the foundation form, which is also the simplest, and then take the next shortest and easiest step. I have always taken the small letter *i* as my fundamental form, and have taught the writing of the alphabet in the following order :

Do not allow the children to try a new letter till they have mastered the one upon which they are working. In this way you will teach writing once for all, and there will be no need of pursuing it as a study in the grammar grades.

MOVEMENT IN WRITING.

Pen writing should be taught just as soon as a child has thoroughly acquired the forms of the letters. It should begin, certainly in the third year, and may begin in the second. This is a purely gymnastic exercise, and, like all gymnastic exercises, position and movement should be acquired by the greatest precision and accuracy. The simple thing to be accomplished in pen writing is, that a perfectly smooth line may be made on the paper by both nibs of the pen. Give very few directions, and follow them strictly. Erect, easy position; both feet squarely planted on the floor; knees at a little more than right angles; forearm on the table; elbow never drawn back of a right angle. Slide on the nail of the fourth or ring-finger. Let the pen rest in the pen fingers (the thumb and first two fingers), the pen-holder opposite the knuckle. Give a great many simple exercises in movement. It is a good plan to perform these exercises to rhythmic movement, regulated by piano-playing. It is of little use to have one position and drill for these gymnastic exercises in writing, and to have another and entirely different one in the regular writing, composition, etc., of the pupil. A few months' thorough work in position and movement, and then rigidly holding pupils to the same in all their writing, will give each child an excellent hand-writing, unless some physical difficulty intervenes.

TALK XII.

TALKING WITH THE PENCIL.

WHEN the child enters the school-room, he comes into a new world, and should bring all that is good and pleasant in his old world with him. The strange surroundings, the new faces, banish from his consciousness almost everything but wonder and fear. If to this is added a teacher strong in discipline, who would put the pupil as soon as possible in the well-worn grooves of order, it is likely that fear and consequent timidity will be the controlling power in the child while he is in school. On the other hand, a warm, affectionate greeting, a cordial shake of the hand, and something to do or see that is pleasant, from the moment that he comes into the school-room, will drive away his fears, and allow his own nature and his own knowledge and skill to have free course. Give a child something to do the moment he enters the school-room. A piece of chalk to work on the board, a slate and pencil, a pile of blocks; anything to attract his attention. Lead the child to talk as freely in the school-room as he does at home. He has learned idioms, pronunciation, accent, use of language, by imitation. Continue this process of imitation by exercises in imitating the voice of the teacher. Have him pronounce sentences, suiting the words to the action, thus, — teacher stands before the class and says (holding up her right hand), "This is my right hand," the children do the same; "This is my left hand," "I can stand up," "See me stand up," "I can run," "I can walk," "I can jump," "I can skip," etc.; always uttering the word as the action is performed. Then have pupils review. Ask them how many things they can do; and have one pupil after another perform acts, and tell at the same time what they are doing. Let the teacher point to objects and say, "There is the clock," "There is a picture," and have the pupils imitate her. Use *here, there, this, those*, in the same way. Place objects in different positions, and have pupils tell where they are. Introduce the easiest object lessons. Lead pupils to tell what they see, in the simplest possible way. Plants, stuffed animals, and other objects of the kind may be used with good effect. Lessons in Form and Color, and in fact all the lessons laid down in the Manuals of Object Teaching, may be used as helps for the teacher, if she allows the child to see for himself, and use his own language in talking. Pictures may be used in the same way. The great purpose should be to train the child to talk freely and correctly. It is a good plan to note down all the idioms a child has at his command. Faults in pronunciation should be corrected by repetition of the right pronunciation. Faults in articulation should be carefully corrected, by leading the child to place the organs of speech in the proper positions. Until the child talks with a good degree of freedom, little or no effort should be made to change the incorrect use of language. After this important period is passed, pupils should not be allowed to use ungrammatical forms. The simple remedy for inaccurate habits of speech is to give the child many opportunities to use proper sentences. This should be done almost invariably with objects. If, for instance, the child uses *is* for *are*, lead the child to talk about numbers of objects before him, using the word *are*. You will remember that I said that all new idioms should be learned in the oral language, and not in the written. All the modifications of subject and predicate may be taught objectively. For instance, the adverbs and adjectives. Objects may be placed in different positions,—for example, a hat upon the table,—and the question asked, " Where is the hat ?" All the prepositions may be taught in this manner. Degrees of comparison may be taught by comparing objects. " This is a little block," " That block is larger than this," " This block is the largest." Adjectives may be taught by leading the child to see the qualities of objects.

When the child or a group of children has been trained to observe attentively, and to talk fluently, the work of teaching Reading may profitably be begun. It is generally an extravagant use of time to begin Reading before this power is acquired. When teachers fully comprehend that education is the generation of power, they will know better how to adapt the steps of progress to the mind's ability. Haste makes a terrible waste, when it consists in taxing the child's strength in an undue degree. I have given in a former talk the method by which I would teach Spelling. The first year should be spent in training the child to copy (in sentences) all the words he learns in reading, with absolute accuracy. The beginning of the second year dictation may be given. I wish to repeat here two rules for Spelling, that should be invariably followed. First, train the children to know when they don't know a word. The teacher should write words which the children do not know on the blackboard, until they are able to use the dictionary. Second, never allow a child to write a word incorrectly, or see a word incorrectly spelled, if it be possible to prevent it. When it is found that pupils can write from dictation all the words they have previously used in copying, the Talking with the Pencil should begin.

TALK XIII.

TALKING WITH THE PENCIL, CONTINUED.

ALL education consists of the development of thought and expression. The thought must precede the expression. Thought, as I have explained, is the relation of ideas. The best stimulus the child can have for clear thought is the observation of objects in relation. The simplest way to bring thought into the mind, in order to express it with the pencil, is to perform some simple act. Let the teacher take up, for example, a block, and ask, "What did I do?" "Tell me upon your slates what I did," and have pupils write an appropriate sentence, each writing it in his own way. Let the teacher sit down in a chair; stand up; walk; run; reach; laugh; sing; shake hands; rap on the table; point to the clock; and perform a thousand simple acts, and have pupils tell with their pencils what she has done. Let a pupil perform an act, and have the others describe it with their pencils. Let two pupils plan, and do, something for their playmates to describe. In this way all the idioms that a child uses, and even new idioms, may be introduced. Pupils may be led to use the various modifications of subject and predicate in single words (adjectives or adverbs), phrases, and clauses. Prepositions may be taught in the written language, as they were in the oral, by placing objects in different positions. Adverbs, by modifying actions, as, walking *slowly*, and *swiftly*, etc. In fact, all the ways I have just given for oral work may be used in the written. Pictures may be effectively used. Every teacher should have a large collection of good pictures. These may be cut out of illustrated books and papers, and pasted upon stout cardboard. Let each child take a picture, and write upon the slate one thing that he sees in the picture. After he has done that well, let him write another and another. Great care should be taken to train children to write sentences ; using the proper capitals and punctuation. This can be done only by having them write a great number of single sentences. They should not be allowed to write connected sentences, until they have formed the habit of beginning and ending the sentences properly. Teachers will often allow children to write a whole page without the proper separation of sentences one from the other, repeating "and" and other words over and over again. This is simply leading them into bad habits. A good way to prevent this is to require pupils to ask and answer questions, writing both question and answer. Pictures may be used in a great many ways. Write questions on the board, to aid the pupils—such as, "What things do you see in the picture?" "Where are they?" "What are they doing?" "What have they been doing?" "What do you think they will do?" "What are the names of the persons in the picture?" [*Note.*—Let pupils give names according to their own fancy.] These and many other questions may be asked to stimulate investigation. When the proper time arrives—that is, when pupils can write single sentences correctly—have them describe the picture fully ; and then have them imagine and write a story about the picture. This they will do with great pleasure. From the first, children should be trained to tell, in their own language, what they have read ; either at the close of the lesson, or at the beginning of the succeeding lesson. When they begin to talk with the pencil, after each lesson in reading, let them go to their seats and write one thing they have read. Follow this by two things, then three, then four ; and at last have them write all they can remember.

Objects may be used as the best means of training children to talk with the pencil. I wish to say a word here about object teaching. That object teaching which tries to force a child to see all the teacher sees in an object, or has prepared, by copying a schedule of things to be seen from a Manual of Object Teaching, and then leads the child to use a lot of strange words, like "opaque," "transparent," "flexible," etc., at the same time he is struggling to observe ; is to my mind as completely wrong as the old-fashioned text-book rote learning. In the first place, the whole attention should be directed to the observation of the object, without being encumbered by new words. Secondly, the child can see very little in the object at first. The attempt to make him see that which the mature mind only has the power to observe, is manifestly wrong. The rule to be followed is—place the object before the child, let him see what he can, and write what he sees. Then by questioning and devices lead him to see more.

Follow the child, and not make the child follow you. Thus, gradually and naturally, the child's powers of observation will develop. In other words, the object should ask the questions, and the child should answer them.

Natural objects are the very best means of training the observing faculties ; and at the same time the child can be led to acquire the elementary facts or a, b, c's of Science. Seeds sown on brown paper, or in cotton, their germination and growth watched, and every change noted by the children, on paper or slate, may be used to arouse the greatest curiosity, and at the same time to teach language in a very effective way. Plants inside of the room, and out-of-doors shrubs, trees, and flowers, should be made the subjects of object and language lessons. I trust that I shall live to see the day, when both Reading and Composition will be beautifully taught by the inspiring stimulus of facts, gained from natural objects, that will lay a grand foundation for a future knowledge of all the Natural Sciences.

All lessons in objects, form, and color, should be made language lessons. The highest perfection of composition is reached in accurate descriptions of objects. Toward this end all teaching of language should steadily tend, without the slightest forcing or overdriving.

Every teacher should be a good story-teller. By constant practice, she should be able to tell a story in a clear, simple, concise manner. Hans Christian Andersen's, Grimm's, and Hebel's charming stories may be told by the teacher, and then written out by the pupil.

In conclusion, there are certain important rules to be observed at every step. First, always be sure that the thought is in the mind before you ask the pupil to express it. Second, never allow any careless work; never permit a pupil to write a word or sentence wrong, as I have said, if it be possible to prevent it. It is a good plan for the teacher to move around among her pupils while they are writing, and closely watch all they are doing. Erase every mistake, and have pupils try again. Such expressions as, "You do not see well," "I am glad you see something in the picture" (or the object), "Look again, and look closer," "Be very careful while you are writing that word," may be used by the teacher with good effect. Third, have pupils *read* everything they write. Pupils may read each other's stories. Use ruled brown paper freely in writing. When pupils get command of the pen, have them use ink in writing their stories.

If this plan of training pupils to talk with their pencils, which I have tried to outline, be closely followed, I am quite sure, from my experience, that every child of ordinary ability may be trained to write accurately and rapidly page after page of good English in three years. And, above all, they may be trained to talk with their pencils with as much eagerness and pleasure as they talk with their tongues. But the best result is not found in correct expression, but in the power to think.

TALK XIV.

COMPOSITION.

In the previous talk, I tried to show how children may be trained in three years to write legibly, correctly, and rapidly a page of English; that good, patient, careful teaching and training will lead them to talk with the pencil as correctly and fluently as with the tongue. The greatest result is that they love to do this work, and that they are entirely prepared by a thoroughly formed habit, ever after to express whatever thoughts they may have in good English. Education consists, primarily, in the development of thought and expression. Expression is used by the true teacher simply and solely as a means of knowing just how and what the pupil thinks, in order to lead him to higher struggles and greater victories. I am aware that most so-called teaching consists in the training of expression without regard to thought—that is, the child's imitative powers alone are cultivated, while his creative strength is left to pine and wither under a mass of meaningless words. If the teaching is real teaching—*i. e.*, thought development—all the studies that now follow (after the third year), Geography, Arithmetic, and the Sciences, may be made the best kinds of language lessons. Every real lesson is carefully planned and given to evolve thought. The child's previous training has given him the power to give to the teacher all the thought evolved, either orally, or in writing. During the lesson the thought is given orally; when it is finished it should invariably be given to the teacher in writing. All true up-building of any science consists of logical premises, sequences, and conclusions. Each step grows out of the consistent union of all previous thought of which each lesson is a constituent part. It holds true, then, that if the thought evolved in the pupil's mind be logical, its expression, either orally or in writing will be—that is, real teaching, assisted by constant written expression, must train a child into the highest art of written composition.

There is little or no necessity of going outside of the regular branches for the best kind of language teaching. Elementary Geography furnishes an exceedingly fruitful source for charming written descriptions of hills, valleys, plains, coast lines, bays, gulfs, rivers, springs, in fact all the forms of water and land under the pupil's observation, which alone can give the power of imagining all unseen forms of land and water. When these unseen forms are moulded and described, and the great, magnificent unseen world is imaged through and by the seen, all these creations of the imagination will make inspiring subjects for composition.

Take one step farther, and from the earth spring the countless forms of vegetation. Trees, plants, and flowers may be described by the child, and each description be an inspiration to further observation.

The animals may be described by the quick pens of the children. Shelter, clothing, cities, commerce, and all the interesting subjects with which Geography fairly teems, form an exhaustless source of excellent themes. Faith, Hope, and Charity may be left to repose serenely in the lists of subjects for compositions, until they have time to bud and blossom in the child's heart.

History, so closely allied and growing out of Geography, if properly taught, may be made a most excellent means of language teaching. Pictures, illustrating the great events in history, may be described. Following this, the teacher should tell short, interesting stories in history, which may be given back by the ready writers. Then comes a carefully arranged list of topics in History. The school library, if teachers and school committees have done their duty, is rich with historical works, adapted to the capacity of children. The village or city library also, is at their command. The eager children are led to read up the topic in a large number of excellent books. In the hour of recitation, they pour out their new-found treasures for their schoolmates to hear and discuss, and for the teacher to mould into consistency and order. Then comes the happy time when they can tell the whole story in their own words, on clean sheets of white paper. I am describing no Utopia, but a reality, that comes to those who have an immense faith in the capabilities of human development. Every pupil in a grammar school, at the end of an eight years' course, may be trained to do this beautiful work. You who, instead of feeding the child's wonderful exhaustless power of imagining the good, the true, and the beautiful, driven where the cutting lash of tradition turns the grand study of history into a dry, stupid rote-learning of pages, dates, and meaningless generalizations, will remember that the New Education leads you to the heights beyond Jordan, within sight of the Promised Land. Do not turn back to the rocky, sandy desert of Sin.

Arithmetic, if it be the study of numbers of things, instead of figures, has for its purpose the development of exact logic. And if the logic is exact, the statements and rules and definitions must be. The pupils are led to discover every fact, process, and generalization for themselves, and then to state what they have discovered in concise language. Thus Arithmetic may be made to fill an indispensable place in language training.

I have spoken of the use of the elements of Natural Science as an excellent means of language teaching. From what I have already said, you will see that each step in the teaching of Science may be materially assisted by written descriptions. There are teachers who stoutly aver that the child can spend weeks and months, and even years, upon the study of columns of words in that expressionless volume called the Spelling-book. Now, I would like to ask, if the pupil writes, and writes correctly, day after day all the words he learns in History, Geography, Arithmetic, and the Natural Sciences, how many more words does he need to learn? What is the use of the Spelling-book?

When should Grammar be taught? After the facts necessary to the metaphysical generalizations, that are indispensable for the comprehension of the difficult science of language. When the mind is ready to use a high form of logical deduction. What is the use of

Grammar? First, to enable the mind to look more closely into the masterpieces of composition, in such a way as to comprehend the thought of an author in all its fulness and completeness; second, to express thought orally and in writing, in the clearest, most concise, and beautiful manner. Correct speaking and correct writing can only be learned by constantly speaking and writing correctly. No incorrect form should ever be presented to pupils until they reach the age of careful reflection. The custom of writing incorrect syntax for children to correct, is a vicious one. Many teachers who are now breaking away from the cast-iron method of teaching, parsing, and analysis, are diluting the old forms by an infusion of weaker ones—*i. e.*, they are training children to use words for the sake of using them, without regard to the thought that should always inspire their use. They lead children to make sentences, using "are," "is, ' "been," etc., just (as I have said) for the purpose of using the word. Now, if the child is continually writing, from the second year to the eighth inclusive, and every sentence is written under the stimulus of thought, he will use all the necessary words correctly, and repeatedly. There is, therefore, little or no need of purely word lessons. But this teaching of grammar is infinitely better than the old way of taking a sentence, that was made to express a beautiful thought, or behind which lies a grand picture; and mangling it by hard names, cutting it into minute pieces, hanging its mutilated remains on cruel diagrams; while the author's meaning remains as far away from the pupil's mind as the bright stars in heaven. There will come a time, in the course of proper development, when teaching technical grammar may be made a most excellent and profitable study; when the rich mines of thought and emotion, of which our literature is full, may be opened to the growing minds of children. Technical grammar, to my mind, as it is usually taught, effectually disgusts children, and bars the way to deeper insight into the beauty and strength of language.

TALK XV.

NUMBER.

AT the outset of this discussion, three questions should be very carefully answered: What is number? What can be done with numbers? What are the uses of number? It is of the utmost importance that we know definitely and exactly the nature of the subject we teach; its relations to other subjects; its place as a means of mental development; and its utility in the affairs of life. If the correct definition of the subject be not entirely comprehended, all attempts at teaching will be vague and unsatisfactory. The usual definitions of number are open to criticism; for instance, "A number is a collection of units." A collection of objects of the same kind may be designated as a *few*, *several*, *some*, etc. Thus you see the definition fails in definiteness. The best way to define anything is to concentrate the mind upon the thing to be defined. I place, for example, several blocks before you. You can say, "There are *some* blocks," "There are *several* blocks," "There are a *few* blocks." "Some," "several," and "few" are adjectives limiting the substantive, "blocks." If you wish to be more definite in regard to a collection of blocks, by a closer inspection you are enabled to say, "There are five blocks." "Five" is also a limiting adjective.

What is the difference between the former limitations of "few," "some," and "several," and of the last, "five"? The difference, you see, is in definiteness of limitation of the collection. "Five" answers definitely the question, "How many blocks?" It is difficult to formulate a satisfactory definition from these facts. The best we can give at present is, that number definitely limits objects of the same kind to how many. The correlative of this definition is, that surfaces, lines, corners, or points definitely limit volumes or bodies of matter in regard to dimensions. You will observe that number definitely limits *objects* of the same kind, in regard to how many. Number limits nothing vague or intangible. Number is not a quality of objects or any part of an object; it simply limits objects of the same kind in one particular way. We can make these limitations first, by the senses; by sight, touch, and hearing. But these limitations of the senses must have their limitations—that is, the visual, tactual, auricular grasp of numbers of things, however highly cultivated, must reach a point beyond which it cannot go. What this point is, I am not at present able to say. Following, and leaving, the point where the sense-grasp ceases, must come what may be called, the grasp of the imagination. The latter depends totally upon the former for its definiteness and distinctness. This fact is of the greatest importance. The unseen can only be measured by the seen. For instance, experience, or, in other words, actual sense products, are the only measures of that which cannot come within the direct and limiting acts of the senses. We measure the unseen mile by the yard or rod that is definitely fixed in the mind by close observation. We measure a hundred things by a standard that has been fixed in the mind in the same way, by the action of the senses.

I have often heard objections raised to the object method of teaching number, because the eye and hand can take in so few things at a time. This objection is illogical to the last degree ; for it is of the utmost importance that our measures of values, that can be obtained only through the senses, be as distinct to the mind as the actual yard-stick or bushel to the measurer. You can easily see how a slight fault in the standard would bring about an immense error in great numbers of things. Precisely in the same way, if the standards of measure are not distinct in the mind, the imagination of numbers of things that lie beyond the sense-grasp, will be weak and wrong. Thus you see that the illogical argument of the objectors to object teaching is, in-reality, the very strongest reason that can be given in favor of such teaching.

What can be done with numbers? I advise you always, for such answers, to observe closely numbers of things. Here are a number of blocks. What can I do with them? In what relations can you see them? Take this one number ; with your eyes you can perceive the definite limitation as to how many. What can I do with this number? I can separate it into other numbers or parts, each of which you limit definitely in your mind by the means of sight. Can I do more? Try it. Here are several numbers. What can be done with them? I unite them into one number.

What more can be done with a number? I separate the number into parts, or other numbers; I unite numbers into one whole number. I can do this actually, or I can think it done. Numbers can be united; a number can be separated. Every operation in arithmetic, however difficult or complex, must consist of one or both of these two simple processes—uniting and separating. There are two relations of numbers, in these two processes, which are severally actual counterparts, or correlatives of each other. These relations may be called, first, the relation of unequal numbers to each other; second, the relation of equal numbers to each other. I can separate this number of blocks into numbers that are not equal, each to the other; I can unite the unequal numbers into one number. I can separate this number into equal numbers or parts; I can unite the equal numbers into one number. Here we have the so-called fundamental four operations of arithmetic. Uniting numbers (or making a unit of them) is addition; uniting equal numbers, a simpler process to the eye and to the imagination than the union of unequal numbers, is multiplication. The reverse of the former is subtraction; of the latter, division. A full comprehension of these simple facts, and the highly important truth, that every operation in arithmetic consists solely and entirely of the application of these simple relations, will make the subject of arithmetic a true science, instead of a complex art.

What is the use of number? First, and the most important point to be understood in the teaching of any subject, is its bearing upon mental development; second, its utility as applied to the affairs of life. The teaching of arithmetic may be divided into two parts: first, training the power to calculate with accuracy and rapidity ; second, the development of the power to reason exactly and logically. When we train a child to add, subtract, multiply, and divide with accuracy and rapidity, the exactness and celerity necessary to good work trains the power of attention. Mathematics is the only exact science ; if the premises are correct, the conclusions must be. To form a strong effectual habit of seeing and thinking of things just as they are, and in their exact relations, is the province of mathematics. There are, then, two motives in teaching arithmetic ; one of which is to train attention, the other, the higher and more important one, is the development of the power to reason logically. All arithmetical reasoning must be done, by bringing the mind to bear directly upon the relations of numbers of things. Language is simply the means of bringing the numbers of things and their relations into the mind.

How shall, or rather how *must* number be taught ? I use this word *must* because, primarily and fundamentally, there is only one way to teach number—that is, by direct observation of numbers of objects. We may, it is true, teach the language of number, leaving the association of the language with the ideas they should recall, to accident, and fondly imagine that we are teaching number. As well might we try to teach the facts in botany without plants, in zoölogy without animals, form without forms, and color without colors, as to teach number without numbers of objects. All primary ideas of number and their relations, must be obtained immediately through the senses, and by their repeated limitations as numbers of things, as to how many.

The first step in teaching number is, to ascertain, by careful examination, just how much the child knows of number—*i.e.*, just his acquired power of limiting of objects of the same kind, to how many; just how many limitations of this kind he has acquired. His knowledge of number, has been acquired through some necessity of limiting the number of objects he handles or sees. Thus a child in the kindergarten, who is constantly handling objects — splints, pieces of paper, blocks, etc., placing them in different forms, such as triangles, squares, oblongs, &c., is gaining unconsciously, in the best possible way, knowledge of number. The child's real knowledge of number, consists in recognizing numbers of things at sight. Ability to count must not be confounded with the true knowledge of numbers of things. Counting is generally ordinal; his four or five is apt to be nothing but the fourth or fifth. Just what he does know, is the first question to be answered by the teacher. He may know numbers without knowing their names or the words that recall them. It would not be fair, then, to gauge his knowledge of number, by asking him to bring you *three*, *four*, or more things. Hold up three objects and say, "Bring me so many," is the first and easiest test. If this test is successful, hold up a number of objects (not more than four), and say, "Bring me—" [naming the number]. Third test, hold up a number of objects and ask, "How many?" Fourth, request the child to bring you so many, giving the number without showing the object.

When you have ascertained just what the child knows of number, begin there. From repeated tests, given by myself, and by teachers under my supervision, the average child of five, or even six years of age, does not know three, when he enters the school-room. The reason for this, as I have before intimated, is not far to seek. It can be found in the fact, that he has not been led to limit objects in the definite way required by number. The teacher should know exactly the facts that the child must acquire in order to know number comprehensively. That is, just what separations and unions of numbers cover the whole ground. These facts can be briefly stated thus: First, the equal numbers in a number, the equal numbers that make a number; second, the equal parts of a number; and third, any two unequal numbers in a number, and any two unequal numbers that make a number. This applies to numbers from one to twenty inclusive. These facts should be recognized by the child, *without the slightest hesitation*, on the presentation of objects, and should be recalled in the same manner, on hearing, or seeing the language that represents them. I wish to emphasize this point, that the facts should be known without the slightest hesitation. That which is learned should be sunk into automatic action. That teaching which leaves the child a prey to helpless counting of fingers, when he wishes to reach a fact, is very poor indeed. The struggle of education is essentially for freedom—*i.e.*, the mind should be freed by proper repetitions and drill, so that petty details may be left behind, in order that power may be concentrated upon the higher step. For instance, in solving a problem, the whole power of the mind should be brought to bear upon the exact relations of the numbers of things, free entirely from calculation ; because the calculation needed has been so thoroughly mastered, that it becomes secondary and entirely subordinate, requiring simply automatic action. Therefore you will see of what exceeding importance it is, that the facts, step by step, should be thoroughly acquired once, and forever.

TALK XVI.

NUMBER, CONTINUED.

THE almost hopeless confusion in their knowledge of arithmetic, that we find in older pupils, is owing in greater part to the attempt to teach too much during the first year. I have seen, many times, fifty, or even one hundred, laid down in the course of study to be taught. I have tried during the last eleven years, to teach number to little folks; and I have never yet succeeded in teaching, nor have I ever seen *ten*, really taught during the first year. I am well aware that many good teachers argue, that by constant repetition of the language, without regard to what the language expresses, fifty, or even one hundred may be taught—*i.e.*, the child, by unceasing drill may repeat a great quantity of gibberish, that to the casual observer may seem to be a valuable result. Ask these children to verify one of their voluble sentences, by showing the real relations of numbers of things, that the sentence was made to represent, and you see, at once, that they have spent much valuable time in learning an unknown language. The same teachers argue that the child cannot reason, and therefore he must be taught the language, before the things. All this unreason, arises from the attempt, that tradition forces upon us, to teach far more than the child can learn. There is no time in the child's life when he cannot see, judge, generalize, and imagine, providing the work is adapted to his mental capacity. It is this lack of adaptation, which leads to this erratic theory, and ruinous practice. Give the child time to grow, and wait patiently until the germs of power burst out of their fruitful soil of unconsciousness.

Teach each number as a whole, as you teach everything within the sense-grasp. When the idea of a number is in the mind as a whole, the tendency of the mental power awakened, by the whole, is to go to the parts. We can only analyze that which is in the mind. Forced analysis, before the object is clear in the mind, generates weakness. Let the child discover everything he can in a number, and discover it for himself, and by himself. If, for instance, he is learning 4; he has already learned 1, 2, and 3; and by skilful leading he can discover the 1's, the 2's, the 3 and 1, and 1 and 3, he finds in 4.

There are teachers who argue, that an attempt to teach the four operations at the same time, confuses the child. It would, no doubt, if the language alone were learned, without regard to the thought which that language expresses. But let us see. I hold up four blocks, separated into 2's.

What do you see? You say, "Two and two are four," or in other language, "Two twos are four," "There are two twos in four," "Four less two is two." Which fact do you see first? I have never had a class who agreed upon this. I hardly know myself. It is logical to suppose, that we must see the separation, before we can see the combination. No; we must see the whole before the part. It is the old question of trying to separate synthesis from analysis. I am inclined to believe that it is impossible for us to synthesize without analyzing, or *vice versa*. The synthesis of units should sink, as quickly as possible, into unconscious acts and not be kept alive by counting. But I think the proof is positive, that if we see two twos *in* four, we also see [at the same time] that two twos *are* four. That three and two are five, we see at the same time that we do, that five less two is three, and five less three is two. Now, instead of confusing the mind, correlative relations mutually assist each other in comprehending each relation. To spend a long time in adding numbers, without noticing consciously the separations; follow that by a long term of subtracting; after which teach multiplying and dividing; produces, I think, the inextricable confusion regarding number, that I have never failed to find in grammar grade classes. The same theory carried out in botany, would take one part of the plant—the leaves, for instance — and teach that, without regard to the whole plant; and then returning, teach the bark, then the stem, and so on. This manner of teaching belongs, not to a primary, but to a secondary stage of work.

One important point I wish to make very clear to you, because in most English arithmetics, the point has been sadly misunderstood. I have said that the facts to be learned, are; the equal numbers *in* a number, and the equal *parts* of a number. I hold up four blocks; you readily see that there are two twos in four; that one half of four is two. Compare the two twos (2 2's = 4) in four, with, one half of four is two ones (2 1's = 2). Now, in most of the arithmetics published in this country and Great Britain, both of these radically different relations, are represented by one written sentence, viz.; 4 ÷ 2. Arithmetic is an exact science and it is absolutely indispensable that it have an exact language. I cannot conceive why these two relations have been almost totally unrecognized by book-makers. The only way I can account for it is, that the language of arithmetic seems to have arisen from the relations of the signs, and not the numbers of things. Finding the equal parts of a whole number, which I would like to call *partition*, in contradistinction to the equal parts of a unit (fractions), is not, perhaps, one of the simplest processes. But it may successfully begin when the child is learning four, and the two operations of measuring by equal numbers, (division) and finding the equal parts of a number, should be kept entirely distinct from each other, in the child's mind, as they really are, or will be, unless his mind is confused by an ambiguous sentence. Discriminate very sharply between learning number, and learning the language of number. The former must precede the latter. If I am any judge of results, nine tenths of the teaching of arithmetic consists in teaching figures alone, with little or no regard to numbers. This you may easily test by asking pupils to verify with objects a few sentences like these :

$$\tfrac{1}{2} \text{ of } \tfrac{1}{4}, \tfrac{3}{6} \div \tfrac{1}{2}, \text{ etc.}$$

The language of arithmetic is made up of idioms, that have little or no analogy with the rest of the language.

For instance, the word *from*, in subtraction, is used in arithmetic only in the sense of *out of*. *Times*, in multiplication is a misleading word. Bear in mind, then, that in the first steps of teaching number, the ideas of number and their relations are *the things* to be taught. Allow the child to use his own idioms to express what he sees, until the ideas become fixed in the mind. Then gradually introduce, by using them yourself (do not require the pupils to use them at first), the conventional idioms peculiar to arithmetic. Thus, these forms of speech become gradually associated with the thought. There is no danger of using the new terms, when they recall exactly what they mean.

There is another important point in the language of arithmetic. When the child enters school, he has clear ideas of the spoken words, such as "hat," "mat," "cat," "box," etc., with which written words are to be associated. He has been gathering these ideas through five or six years of constant mental exercise, but, as I have shown, he has very few, if any, clear ideas of number. *Ideas grow very slowly.* It takes a long time, with many acts of perception, to fix one idea clearly in the mind. It is of immense importance that these ideas come into the mind so distinctly, that they can be used in thinking. The oral language must be used to assist in gaining the ideas, and to express them. But if we endeavor to teach both forms of language, the written and the oral, at the same time the all-important work of idea growth is going on, do we not try to do too much? Will not the written figures be taken, as they constantly are, for that which they should represent? I would defer the teaching of written figures, for this and other reasons, until at least ten, is thoroughly taught. Then, figures may be taught, as words and sentences in reading are, by associating them directly with that which they represent.

I will now try to give some indications of the step-by-step plan, by which numbers may be taught. First, teach the number as a whole; use a great variety of objects appealing to sight, touch, and hearing; second, lead the child to discover every fact for himself, giving each one a number of objects; third, after the facts have been repeatedly discovered by the child, fix them in the mind by constant drill. Let the child take the number of objects, and show you rapidly, what he can see in it. Show the objects yourself, and have the pupils tell what they see. Then, without objects, question pupils sharply upon the facts, and have them answer without hesitation. Next, apply the numbers learned, in all sorts of practical ways, by means of little problems. Have pupils make problems for themselves. In the teaching of number, use all the common weights, measures, money, that come within the scope of the number taught. Teach one number at a time, and have the pupils learn the facts in that number, before another is taught. Review continually. Judge of your progress by the increasing power of attention on the part of your pupils.

When should we stop using objects? I have but one answer to this question. Cease using any object, when it can be thought of, and used without the presence of the object. This is a general rule, and applies to all object teaching. When children can think of the things, or qualities required for the desired mental action, without the presence of objects, their after-use cultivates weakness rather than strength. That is, when the mind has abstracted the required ideas of number, and their relations, from numbers of objects, then, the real abstract number may be used. The abstract number that cannot be defined, or thought of, is a snare and a delusion, and has caused more vague, meaningless, stupid work in arithmetic, than the teaching of the names of the letters has in reading. We say, for example, that the multiplier is abstract: 2 times 3 means two threes. Two is a limiting adjective, and limits threes. It has a definite meaning, and to say that it is abstract, in the sense given by most arithmetics to that miserable word, is nonsense.

Let me say, in conclusion to this talk, that if you have been, like myself, trained in figure work, instead of the study of number, I should advise you to lay aside, for a time, all you ever thought you knew about arithmetic, and begin its careful, thoughtful study over again, [using numbers of objects all the time], with a little child to lead you.

TALK XVII.

ARITHMETIC.

WHEN ten has been thoroughly taught, begin the teaching of the written language of number. The process of teaching figures, is precisely the same as in teaching written words. First, show a number of objects, and then write (on the blackboard) the sign ; second, write the sign, and ask pupils to show that number of objects ; third, show a number of objects, and have pupils write the sign ; fourth, send the class to the board, then show numbers of objects one after the other, and have pupils write the sign ; fifth, show 111, 11, thus ; then change to 11111, and say, " Write that." They write, " 3 and 2 are 5;" sixth, teacher erases *and*, and writes $+$, *are* and writes $=$. " Now read it the same way as before." Teach the signs, $=$, $+$, $-$, $\times$, $\div$, very carefully, one at a time, and then review, by writing them together. Show objects (as in oral teaching), and have pupils write the answers. Introduce exercises like the following :

1	2	3	4
$8 \div 2 = 4$	$8 \div 2 =$	$8 \div = 4$	$ \div 2 = 4$
$4 2\text{'s} = 8$	$4 2\text{'s} =$	$4 \text{'s} = 8$	$ 2\text{'s} = 8$
$5 + 4 = 9$	$5 + 4 =$	$5 + = 9$	$ + 4 = 9$
$8 - 5 = 3$	$8 - 5 =$	$8 - = 3$	$ - 5 = 3$
$4 \times 2 = 8$	$4 \times 2 =$	$4 \times = 8$	$ \times 2 = 8$

ARITHMETIC.

Then have pupils erase the answers, (see 2) and write the answers rapidly. Have them erase answers again, and read the columns. Have them erase second line, (see 3) then fill up the columns. Have them erase again, and read. Then let them erase the first line, (see 4) and fill in the answers. Use in these exercises, all the forms of stating processes, to be found in arithmetical calculation ; the pupils learning them, by seeing the relations which they express. In division, for example, $8 \div 4 = 2$, $4)\overline{8}(2$, $4)\dfrac{8}{2}$; in multiplication, $2\times 3=6$, $\begin{array}{r}3\\ \underline{2}\\ 6\end{array}$. When these forms are firmly fixed in the mind, give the same exercises, without using objects. From 10 proceed, number by number, to the development of 20, using both oral and written work. For reviews, give an exercise like this (orally), having pupils write out answers upon slates or board, in columns, *without hesitation :* $7+5$; $5+3$; 4's in 12 ; $10-7$; $\frac{1}{3}$ of 9 ; 6×2. Let pupils change slates, and correct ; the teacher reading the answers. Train pupils to make good figures, and to arrange their work neatly upon slates, blackboard, or paper. *Never allow any careless work.*

These exercises, however, form only a part of the work which should be done. The oral and written work should go hand in hand. Calculation should be followed by applied numbers ; using, as in oral work, weights, measures, and money. Have pupils buy and sell, and keep an account of their trades, on slate and paper. Give them a great many little problems, that will test their thinking powers. Have them write their own problems, (language lessons). Write on the board 7+4 ; 3×5 ; ½ of 12 ; 16÷4 ; and have them write problems on their slates, using these numbers and their relations. Write examples for them on the board. Have them read them (reading lessons). A Primary Arithmetic may be introduced, [like the "Franklin"] as a reading book, at this stage. The squares of 2, 3, 4, and 5, may be taught, by drawing the squares on the board. Have children make the tables—multiplication and division ; products not exceeding the number taught. I believe, when 20 is thoroughly taught, and all the facts are known without the slightest hesitation, and when the child has formed the habit of using figures, simply to represent numbers of things, in such a way, that the figures, in any and all of their relations, will readily recall the numbers in their relations ; that more than half of the science of arithmetic, is within the grasp of the pupils. This work should occupy the time, at least, of the first two years. It may be done, I think, in one year, if the pupils have had thorough Kindergarten training.

I have not time to speak of the steps from 20 to 100. For this work, I will refer you to the Arithmetical Charts, soon to be published by Cowperthwait & Co. Three years at least, should be allowed for the thorough teaching of 100.

I am often asked the question, "When should the use of objects cease, in the development of number ; that is, in teaching a new number?" It is clear to my mind, that when pupils can analyze a number, [*i.e.*, find the equal numbers in a number, the equal parts of a

ARITHMETIC. 113

number, any two unequal numbers into which a number can be separated, or that make a number,] without the presence of the objects, the time has come when they should not be used. Whether this be at 10, or 20, I know not. I shall have to teach number, to little children a few years longer, before I shall be able to find this important fact. This rule, however, applies to all teaching. Set the child free as soon as possible; train him to help himself; to use that which is in his mind with the slightest external stimulus; but above all things, be sure that he has the right mental objects to use. These must come in through the senses.

I have tried to give you an outline, of how children may be thoroughly grounded in primary arithmetic. If you fully comprehend, and carry out this plan, very little need be said about higher or Written Arithmetic, as it is usually called. For there is absolutely nothing new to be learned in all arithmetical teaching, except the processes which large numbers involve, such as is found in the additions, multiplications, subtractions, and divisions, which cannot be performed without the use of slate and pencil. All these processes should be discovered by pupils.

The tendency of modern teaching has been, to make very simple things complex and difficult. The application of the science of teaching, will bring us back to the grand simplicity, characteristic of true art. The complexity, of which I speak, can arise in no other way, than from a superficial understanding of arithmetic. That is, it consists in taking the language for the thing, and making rules, and definitions, and terms, which appear entirely new to both teacher and pupil, when they are simply a well-known operation under a new name. I have shown that all that can be done with number, consists totally, of separating and uniting numbers. Hence every subject in arithmetic, whether it be fractions, decimals, percentage, interest, or cube-root—whether the numbers be large or small, is only a simple continuance of what the child has already learned ; a new application of the same thing. Let the teacher follow the great pedagogical rule of Pestalozzi. Teach the idea before the word, the thought before the expression, and all will go well. When a new subject is begun, fractions, for example, let the pupils discover what fractions are, by means of objects ; show them the fractions ; have them write the signs upon the blackboard. Follow the usual course in teaching fractions, and you will readily see that pupils can be led to discover for themselves, a mixed number, by showing them by objects a whole number and a fraction ; an improper fraction, by separating a whole number into equal parts. That the parts must be equal, in order to add or subtract ; and when they are equal, they are added and subtracted precisely like whole numbers ; and so on, step by step, they may be led to see the relation of the different equal parts of units. That is, the thoughts can be evolved, by means of objects, before the sentence is written. If you happen to have a class that have been *through the book*, and know all about fractions, write a simple fraction upon the board, and ask them to verify it with objects, *i.e.*—ask them to show you just what the word or sentence means. In all my experience, I have never failed to

ARITHMETIC.

bring about a commendable degree of humility, which is very useful when turning the minds of the pupils afresh upon an old and almost worn-out subject, that students are apt to imagine they have thoroughly mastered.

I cannot urge you too strongly, as teachers, to go back to the study of the real meaning, of all you think you know about arithmetic. My advice comes from my own experience in trying to teach this subject. Finding that I knew figures well, and not numbers of things, I have been obliged to go back to the objects, in order to find just what the figures in their relations mean. My second reason for this advice is, that I find pupils in advanced grades, unable to reason in arithmetic. Reasoning, let me repeat, *must be* upon things, and not words.

The question has been often asked me, "How much analysis would you have?" By analysis, many teachers mean, the repetition of a set formula that has been learned "by heart." That is, a child learns a pattern, by which all examples of the same kind may be done, with the slightest possible mental action on the part of the learner. This is not analysis, though it is often called by that name. It is pattern-learning, and is simply, imitation carried over into the sacred region of thought development; and it effectually prevents the growing of any original or creative power. Analysis, is the discovery by the thinking powers, of the parts of a whole, which must be, of course, clearly in the mind, before its parts can be mentally seen. Another difficulty in this so-called elaborate analysis is, that it consumes much valuable time. For instance: "If one apple costs three cents, what will four apples cost?" (Child.) "If one apple costs three cents, four apples, will cost four times as many cents as one apple will cost. Therefore, four apples will cost four times three cents. Four times three cents, are twelve cents. Therefore; if one apple costs three cents, four apples will cost twelve cents." I think I have not put in all the words, that can be put into this complex, and useless explanation; still I have tried to illustrate what I have very often heard. The example given, is the application of a general fact, which the child is learning. If the previous work has been correct, all the child needs to say, is, " Twelve cents ;" and go on performing a dozen examples, instead of agonizing over the stiff formula of one. Let me not be misunderstood. The pupil's attention should continually be turned back, upon that which has come into their minds as wholes. We learn the science of arithmetic, not for the purpose of knowing arithmetic, but that the study of the subject may increase mental power. The trouble is, that we fix our minds on the quantity to be learned, and not on the value the things learned, has in mental growth.

Now, there is not one thing in the science of numbers, no definition, rule, or process, that cannot be discovered by the child, under the proper leading of a skilful teacher, who knows what she is teaching. The pupils can discover in this way, every *thought*, the language, of course, must be given them. Definitions, rules, processes, and problems, may be an excellent means of mental growth, if each and all are discovered by the pupils for themselves, and by themselves. They are generally, as learned and applied in the pattern fashion, a great means of concealing thought, and increasing stupidity. *The* arithmetic of the future, will contain, not one rule, definition, or explanation of a process. "Education is the generation of power," "Never do anything for a pupil, that he can be led to do for himself." How often these old truths have been repeated, and still, one of the great evils, if not the greatest, is, that we do too much for the pupils. Instead of leaving them to help, and control themselves, instead of cultivating their powers of attention and concentration, we try to make them the passive, innocent recipients of stores of knowledge, without the movement, on their part, of a mental muscle. Explanation is one of the very best means of preventing mental action.

Train a boy to be an athlete; lift him over every bar, carry him up the ladders, defend him with your fists, and then send him out into the world to fight his own battles ! This is exactly what we do, when we make everything plain by ex*plain*ation. I have heard the objection made by teachers, when I have broached this cardinal doctrine of the New Education, that it takes too much time, to lead a child to discover everything for himself. *Education is the generation of power ;* and the generation of power, in the right way, is the very highest economy of which man can conceive. We learn to do by doing, to hear by hearing, and to think by thinking. We see with all we have seen, we do with all we have done, and we think with all we have thought. The greatest delight of all teaching is, to place the difficulty squarely before the pupils, [generally by means of objects,] and then let them work it out for themselves. If they go wrong, do not tell them they are wrong, but ask the question that will set them right. Time is nothing, when power is growing! Look on this picture, and then on that. A class listening to the verbose explanation of an enthusiastic pourer-out of knowledge, watch their faces as they are repeating a rote-learned definition, rule, or formula, or are waiting for their mothers—I beg your pardon—their teachers, to put the food into their open mouths. Or, if you please, behold this class ; led by a teacher inspired by the thorough knowledge of the subject, who has the thought distinctly in her own mind, who is trying dextrously to lead her class to know what she knows, and is very glad to have them discover something that she doesn't know. One class, solemnly marches to their goal of quantity, under the banner of rewards and punishments, per cents, merits, checks, or the rod. ·The other, all aglow with eagerness and zeal, faces flushed in their earnest desire to discover the truth, fearful that some one will tell them, what they wish to find out for themselves, such children are gathering strength at every step, and learning to do the work the world is most in need of.

My dear teachers, fill yourselves full of the subject you would teach, know its nature, its length, breadth, and depth, and then with the knowledge of the learning child, lead him to discover, step by step, what you have discovered. I promise you, that in such work you will find for yourselves, a mental growth on your own part, that can scarcely be found anywhere else, and an unequalled joy, in leading little ones to fulfil the grand destiny for which God intended them.

TALK XVIII.

GEOGRAPHY.

A DESCRIPTION of the surface of the earth and its inhabitants is, perhaps, as comprehensive a definition of geography as can be found. A description of the surface of the earth, consists of a knowledge of the structure of the outside of this ball on which we live; this structure consisting of slopes, relatively gradual and abrupt, that vary its outline; the surface being not that of a perfectly smooth sphere. This description of the surface is limited, in geography, to the constructed merely, and not the construction. The construction applying to the material, is the realm of geology. We have, in geography, two parts. The first, pertains to the superficial structure; the second, to the people who live, and have lived upon the structure. We have, then, the stage and the actors. The first, is real, or structural geography, the second, history. For history has to do with all that men have done in the past, and all they are doing at present.

The first work in geography, is to build into the mind, by means of the imagination, the stage, that may afterward be filled with moving and acting human beings. We can teach geography by means of maps, so that the mind will rarely go beyond the map, *i.e.*, the world and all it contains, is limited to the colored surface of a piece of paper. Now the map, like a word, should be the means of recalling a reality. That teaching of geography, which does not take the student beyond the representation of that which is represented, is manifestly wrong. The description, as I have said, of the surface of the earth, must be of mental pictures of the forms raised above a perfectly level surface. If the surface of the continent were like that of the ocean, [of water], a particular description of surface would be impossible. Varying outlines, then, make it possible for us to describe the surface of the earth. A description of the various and varying forms, that rise above the level of the ocean, is, *per se*, a description of the earth's surface. This description has been almost entirely overlooked, in the study of geography.

The structure of the earth's surface should be studied, just as any other structure or form is studied. Were I to ask you to describe a house that you have seen, you would immediately concentrate your mind upon a mental picture of that house. You would tell me of its height, its roof, its general form, of its doors and windows, and so on. Just in this way, a continental structure may, and should be, described. These varying forms of vertical structure, in their relations, give the character to a continent or any of its parts. Let us look at this a moment, in relation to memory. All that we remember must be located in space, real or imaginary. The more distinct the locality is, in the mind, the more tenaciously and clearly the mind holds any fact in relation to the locality. The more character there is, the more pronounced and varying the slopes, into hills, valleys, coast-lines, and rivers, the easier it is, to fill such localities with facts, and retain them. Our knowledge of locality, upon smooth surfaces, like the ocean, is very vague, hanging as it does upon imaginary lines, drawn from the sun, moon, and stars. I can make my meaning plain, by referring to the method of the modern historian, or novelist. The first thing to be done, on the part of either, when a book is to be written, is to carefully prepare the *terrain* upon which their figures have moved, or are to move. Curtius, the famous historian of Greece, has given us in the first pages of his history, a clear picture of that wonderful peninsula. When one can travel, in imagination, all over that country, can see Thermopylæ, and Marathon, can climb the Acropolis, or wander over the Isthmus of Corinth, can view Sparta in all its surroundings, he is, in a measure, ready to follow the fascinating movements of the characters, either real or imaginary, from Hercules to Bozzaris. The novelist, with a freer pen, and more fanciful range of thought, is wont to describe minutely the landscape, upon which he designs to place his characters. Test yourselves in this respect, and you will see better what I mean. Recall the farm upon which you were born [if you were so fortunate], or any other scene that is fixed in your mind by long familiarity. How from each tree, running stream, valley, or hill, start thousands of recollections, bound to them by the great law of association. Were I to tell you that such and such changes had been made, a house built here, a road there, how quickly would your imagination make a picture of the changes, and these pictures would thereafter be held firmly in your memory. Now, what the novelists and historians do, in order to make us remember their stories and histories, should be done with the structure of the whole earth, and for the same purpose. So that cities, political divisions, the movements of men, and all that is continually moving and changing, may be retained and held, in the forms and spaces that do not change. My first argument, then, for the teaching of structural geography, is, that it is an essential and fixed basis for the memory of eternally changing facts.

The character of the vertical forms of continents determines their horizontal shape or outline. This is plainly seen in the relations of highlands to the seacoast. The vertical forms, also determine the drainage of a continent. The immense uplifted masses may be called the bones, or framework, the drainage, the lifeblood of continental forms. The soft earth or soil, worn away from rocks, that gives us fertile or arable land, is deposited by the drainage of varying slopes. Thus, you see, with the exception of the important element of climate, the structure limits the occupation, resources of food, shelter, clothing, and health of man. The character of mankind depends, to an immense degree, upon the character and position of these structural forms. Compare North America with Africa. The one, with great mountain masses, sloping gradually down to lower levels, and then to the sea ; with its great navigable rivers, and accessible coast ; the other, with mountain masses, to be sure, but with no extensive gradual slopes, so that its rivers to gain their outlets must break through plateaus, thus obstructing navigation ; and we have a picture of two widely different continental forms. They are the extremes. One, with the conditions for steadily moving arterial blood, like the horse ; the other, for the stagnation and slowness of the tortoise. The greatness of nations, may be traced directly to the structural forms upon which they lived and thrived. Egypt, with its narrow strip of very fertile land, fed by the Nile, and bounded by vast deserts, to keep off invaders. Palestine is a natural fortress, with its great wall on the Jordan side, its rocky desert on the south, but with one weak point, the fatal plain of Esdraelon. Had that great rift in the earth's crust, extending from the sea of Galilee to the Dead Sea, never been made, the history of that wonderful and powerful nation, that gave us the foundation for our religion, never would have been. The Grecian Peninsula, had all the conditions for the development of its wonderful history.

The study of the structure of the earth's surface, forms the natural basis of the study of all other Physical Sciences. A knowledge of the surface, is the elementary study of the crust of the earth, and leads directly to Geology, and that to Mineralogy. Drainage, determines the soil, and upon soil and climate depends vegetation ; thus leading directly to Botany. Upon the vegetation depends animal life, the study of which gives us the science of Zoology. The movements and phenomena pertaining to structure, give us both Physics and Physical Geography ; the measurement of form and movement of the earth, Mathematical Geography ; its parts and composition, Chemistry. All these sciences are the direct outgrowth of structural geography. Structural geography, then, may be called the elementary science, upon which all other sciences are founded. This branch has hitherto been almost entirely overlooked or neglected. Indeed, I am obliged to invent a new name for this new science—Structural Geography.

Humboldt, by his careful observations and generalizations, made it possible for Carl Ritter to discover a science of geography. The study of geography, previous to Ritter's time, consisted of the learning of a conglomerated mass of isolated and disconnected facts, that must be held in the mind by the sheer force of verbal memory. The progress of the new science has been, and is, exceedingly slow. Guyot, the pupil and disciple of Ritter, made for us his unequalled Common School Geography. But the book has been a failure, and is now out of print, because teachers who had been taught in the old way could not comprehend its great beauty.

TALK XIX.

GEOGRAPHY, CONTINUED.

IN my last talk, I tried to show that structural geography is the true basis of geographical and historical knowledge. I shall endeavor to show, in this talk, how it should be taught. The purpose is, to fix in the mind, clear, comprehensive pictures of the forms of continents. These forms are made up of slopes. The slopes range from the gradual [level plains], to the most abrupt, [mountains]. These forms, of course, cannot be seen, and the question is, How can they be brought into, or built in the mind? All we know of the unseen must be known by the mental power we call imagination. The law by which the imagination acts is very plain. There is no disagreement among psychologists concerning it. Imagination, is that power of the mind which combines and arranges, with more or less symmetry and proportion, that which primarily comes into the mind through the senses. Every thing imagined, is made up of parts already in the mind, when the particular act of the imagination takes place. All our power of imagining, is absolutely limited to sense products, already the property of the mind that imagines. If you have never thought of this, a very little reflection will convince you of its truth. Try to imagine anything, and then, by analysis, notice if any of the parts are not things you have already known. The unseen is made, or imagined, entirely out of the seen. The question, then, in teaching structural geography, is, How can the proper sense products, necessary to the imaging of the forms of continents, be brought into the mind? The answer is near at hand. In order to imagine the unseen, that which can be seen must be brought clearly into the mind. Elementary geography consists of the close and careful observation of the forms of the earth's surface around us. There is hardly a town or district in the Atlantic States, where each and all of these forms may not be observed.

Higher than mere acquisition of knowledge, geography is the very best means for developing the powers of imagination. Next to the direct action of the senses, imagination is the most important, in its length, breadth, and depth, of all other mental powers. Distinct and true creatures of the imagination, are an indispensable basis for reason, and for ethical and spiritual culture. No subject is more neglected in our schools. 'The little child soon creates a new world out of the scant material of his limited sense products. In this world of fancy, he lives and revels. The child's life would be a sad one, were it not for his own bright, self-created world. The little girl sees a beautiful doll in a stick and a rag. Out of a few broken pieces of crockery and a shingle or two, she creates an elegant pantry. A cane, to the little boy, is a splendid charger. Fairy stories delight all children, and often contain more truth than maxims or precepts. Our Common School education has a tendency to crush out all imagination, or force it into wrong and vicious channels. This steady and strong tendency of the mind, may be developed into an immense power, and geography furnishes, as I have said, one of the very best means for its development.

The first steps in geography, should give the child the means to imagine that which he cannot see. Begin with the forms around you; the close and careful study of the chains or ranges of hills, valleys, plains, coast-lines, springs, brooks, rivers, ponds, lakes, islands, and peninsulas. Study them as you do objects in Botany or Zoology. Take the children out into the fields and valleys; return to the school-room; let them describe orally what they have seen; then mould and draw it; and, finally, have them describe the objects they have seen by writing. Teach them distance by actual measurement; boundaries by fences, and other limitations; drainage by gutters, and the flow of water after a rain. Let them find springs, and discover how the water comes out of the ground. Have them bring in different kinds of earth—gravel, sand, clay, and loam. I have not time to give you any regular order of subjects—if there be one. Begin with one object, study it carefully, then take another, and combine the two, and so on. I wish to call your attention, especially, to the three great means of thought expression. First, the concrete expression; second, drawing; third, language. The first may be done by moulding sand obtained from an iron foundry. Have pupils tell you what they have seen, by moulding the form. Second, have them draw everything they see, in relief, and horizontally. Third, describe what they have seen, orally, and then in writing. Use these means *continually* in teaching geography.

The observation of objects should begin, of course, as soon as the child enters school. The objects around the school-house should be observed : yards, fences, gardens, gutters, roads, fields, pastures, hills, valleys. Out of these objects, many very interesting and profitable object and language lessons may be made. But the teaching of elementary geography proper should not begin much before the fifth year of the child's school life. The work of which I have just spoken, the study of geographical forms that may be observed, should be begun the latter part of the fourth year, or the first of the fifth. One year, at least, should be spent in this study. Parallel with it, books, like, Each and All, Seven Little Sisters, Guyot's Introduction, may be read with great profit. They seem to excite curiosity and inspire the imagination. The power of imagination should be developed at every step. Thus, after a lesson upon the hill, tell the children about the great mountains in the world. When they have seen one river, tell them about others that they can't see. When they have examined, moulded, drawn, and written a description of one peninsula, draw other peninsulas, like Spain, Italy, Greece, Florida, Norway and Sweden, for them. When they have studied an island, tell them about the great islands [the continents].

Constantly excite their curiosity to solve problems like these—Where does the water go, when it falls on the ground ? How far down does it go ? What does it do in the earth? When does it come out of the ground? Where is the more water, in rivers and lakes, or in the ground? Why does not a river run in a straight line? What turns it? Why is it narrow at some places and wide at others? Take the water out of a lake, and what would you have left? What, then, is a lake? Where does a river get its water? How much land does a river drain? What is the difference between a river and a canal? What if the earth was all level, like the floor? What are the uses of a river? a hill? a plain? a valley? When does the water come into the land on the coast? What makes a pebble? What is the difference between a pebble and a grain of sand? a pebble and a great piece of rock? and a quarry? These and other questions, when skilfully used, and the child is led to discover everything for himself, may be made a source of deep and abiding interest on the part of children. The philosophy of geography may begin, as soon as the child can make the slightest generalization.

When the child has in his mind, the necessary sense products, he may begin to build the continents, as the next simplest step. The pupil can be led to imagine the continent, far easier than he can be led to imagine any part of it. Strange as it may seem at first thought, an entire continent is simpler, in its general construction, than a single town or district. It is a mistake, then, to begin with states and sections, before the entire continent is imagined.

There is a common rule in teaching geography, which leads to the teaching of the immediate surroundings of the school-house, the district, the town, the county, the state. This order is illogical, because the county is more difficult to imagine, as I have said, than the entire continent. The reason why we teach the surroundings is misunderstood. The purpose of teaching that which can be seen and examined, is simply and solely, to enable the child to imagine the unseen. The great highlands, long slopes, and regular vertical forms of the whole continent, is, to my mind, the next simplest step, when the facts of elementary geography are in the child's mind.

Another pedagogical rule is often wrongly applied: Begin with the whole, and go to the parts. Thus, many teachers think that the whole must be the great globe itself. The rule should be changed to: Begin with any whole that is in the mind, and go to the parts. Now, there are two kinds of wholes. One is the whole of sense grasp; the other is the whole of the imagination. The latter depends entirely, as I have tried to show, upon the former. Not until the child has the acquired power of imaging or synthesizing the whole continent, is he able to analyze or even think of the parts; how much less is he able to imagine the great round ball we call the earth! The reasonable road to this knowledge is, first, sense products of geographical forms; second, whole continents; then, parts of continents; and last, by means of the acquired power of synthesis, the whole globe.

Mathematical geography, then, should be the last geographical subject taught. But from the first to the last, the facts necessary to the teaching of mathematical geography should be picked up all along the line. The seasons, with all their changes of rain and sunshine, snow and ice, dry and wet weather; growth and death of vegetation; heat and cold; the sun and its movements; the moon and stars; when they rise, how they look, what they do; so far as children can observe, should be made the constant subjects of observation. Mark out, on the floor, the limits of the sunbeams as they strike through the window. Do the same thing the next day, at the same hour. Note the difference, and wonder how it all comes about.

Compare this teaching of real geography, that delights children at every step, that trains close observation, lays the foundation for the development of imagination, and forms the elementary steps of all physical sciences, with the rote learning of a mass of dry, disconnected facts, found in the so-called primary geography. Which does the most good? is a question I leave for you to decide.

TALK XX.

GEOGRAPHY, CONTINUED.

When the elementary facts have been carefully gathered, the building of the continents should begin. By building of the continents, I mean, that the teacher should combine the acquired sense products, into a picture of the horizontal and vertical structure of the continent, so that the pupil can travel, in imagination, all over the structure, and mentally see its parts. This picture, at first, is a general one, a bird's-eye view, to be gradually filled up, and intensified in details, by all after-study of the continents. It is to form the mental framework of all the facts that will be afterward learned. In this framework of memory, cities, boundaries, mining and agricultural regions, may be placed and retained. Geography, as commonly taught, leaves out the indispensable conception of upraised forms, and limits the study to the plain surface of a map, using the artificial helps to memory, of color and boundary lines. In this teaching of geography, maps, both plain and relief, together with description, are used simply as aids in imagining the real continent. That is, the mind is to be carried beyond the symbols to the real things themselves.

The general forms of continents are comparatively

simple. In the first teaching, the teacher should try to fix this general form in the mind, with very little attention to details. The body of land we call a continent consists wholly of slopes, bounded by rivers and coast-lines. It may be taken, at first, as one great mass of land raised above the sea. The first division that should be made, is a division into great and lesser upraised masses or highlands. These upraised masses are bounded by coast-lines on one side, and the line of the lowest level between them. The mountain ranges are simply the tops or apexes of these highlands. They form, in themselves, a very small part, comparatively, of the highland masses. Thus, we start from the Mississippi, the line of the lowest level between the eastern and western highlands, and travel west on that which looks like level ground, until we rise seven thousand feet above the sea, before a mountain is seen.

I wish to speak now, of moulding these forms in sand, as an aid to the imagination in getting pictures of the upraised forms. First, let me say, that the moulding, like maps and other means of description, is simply and solely, a help to the imagination. If the mind sticks in the "mud-pie," as it is often called, the mud is of little or no use. The teacher should be constantly carrying the children's minds from the symbol to the symbolized. An objection is often made to relief maps, because they exaggerate heights. It is impossible to represent to the eye the relative heights of the earth's surface. If relief maps are not used, I would like to ask the objectors, What means have you of leading the pupils to imagine continental forms? As the mind is led from the relief to the reality, when extent can be imagined, the relative heights will take their true place. A board, or table, 3 × 4 feet, with raised edges; half a barrel of sifted foundry sand, dampened so that it can be easily worked with the hands, is material enough for moulding. A few weeks' practice on your part, will enable you to mould any continental form with a considerable degree of skill.

You may begin in several ways. I should begin with the continent that has the simplest form—South America. Throw up the great highlands, that extend from the Straits of Magellan to Panama. Lead pupils to see how the highland determines the outline of the western coast. Compare the abrupt slope on one side, with the long and gradual slope on the other. Lead them to see that, if the western coast is determined by the highlands, the eastern coast must also be so determined. That, if there were no other highlands, the waters of the Atlantic would cut into the land, so as to form two abrupt slopes on either side. Now, the lesser highlands of Brazil, and Guiana may be thrown up, and the pupils will readily see what determines the outline of the eastern coast. Next, from the simple laws of drainage they have already learned, they will be able to locate the great river basins. The different degrees of fertility may also be discovered in the same way. Have each pupil mould the continent. For this purpose, small pieces of board with raised edges may be used, or shallow tin pans, that can be placed on their desks. The discussions of the effect of the form, upon drainage, soil, and vegetation, should go on, hand in hand with the moulding. The outline of the continent may be drawn from the moulded form, and the great highlands and rivers designated. Drawing should be constantly used, from the beginning to the end of all geographical and historical teaching. The aim should not be to draw nice, accurate maps, but to express thought in a rapid way. The first thing, in all description in geography or history, should be, a map of the country or section under study.

When the general form of one continent has been moulded, drawn, and studied, take the next in order of simplicity—North America. When North America has been moulded, the two continents should be compared. First, lead pupils to discover the resemblances between them; then the differences. Have them drawn and moulded, in their relative position. Lead pupils to trace the great highland mass, from Patagonia to Alaska. Follow this with the moulding of Africa. By comparing this continent with North and South America, pupils may be led to discover the causes of the wonderful differences in their history, and development. They can reason from cause to effect, and by such reasoning, discover what an immense influence structure has upon civilization. Asia and Europe, followed by Australia, may be successively moulded and drawn. The comparisons should be constantly made. All the moulding and drawing, should be on a scale of distances, which will develop the power of judging extent. The continents should be located on the globe, so that their relative positions may be seen, and the proper preparation made for the study of mathematical geography. The principal islands and groups of islands, should be studied in the same way as the continents. The continental islands may be discovered as broken fragments of the mainland.

With this study of continental forms, descriptions of vegetation, climate, soil and peoples, should go on ; not in a definite and particular way, but enough should be given to feed the imagination, to arouse curiosity, and clothe the dry bones of the structure with the warm coloring of living forms. Children should read travels, bits of history, etc., in connection with this work of moulding and drawing.

TALK XXI.

GEOGRAPHY, CONCLUDED.

WE have now the general picture of the great land masses that rise above the sea. The pupil can recall them, can travel over them in imagination. With the placing of the continents in their relative positions on the globe, some conception of climate may be taught. Locating the great rivers and their basins, has brought the children to the study of drainage ; and this, in turn, has furnished a basis to the study of vegetation. The soil, and great staple productions of all the continents, may be now learned quicker and better, than the soil and productions of a single country, in the old way, of memorizing facts, which were the staple products of the old geographies. All the maps of the continents may be drawn upon the board in their relative positions, as they appear on the Mercator Projection. The soil may be divided into fertile, arable, and barren, and indicated by colored crayons upon the maps. Lessons upon soil should be given, and specimens of the various kinds of earth, from gravel to vegetable mould, examined. If you have a bit of ground near the schoolhouse, raise all the different kinds of useful plants that you can. Then, take up successively all the great food staples. Locate the wheat, the rice, the corn, the potato, and the rye regions, and indicate them, as I have said, in colors on the maps. Follow these, with the luxuries in the way of food—coffee, tea, cocoa, etc. Then the subject of shelter and fuel may be studied, the forests and kinds of wood. Lessons should be given upon specimens of wood. Plants used for clothing may come next; the cotton and flax, the caoutchouc, etc., may be located. This study of plants, as I have said, leads us directly to the study of Botany.

From vegetation they may go to animals. These may be classified, and their haunts discovered; animals for food, animals for clothing, beasts of burden, domestic and wild animals. This distribution may be noted, by drawing the animals on the maps, as they are distributed over the surface of the earth. You will readily see that, by this work, you have created a necessity for the study of Zoology.

Next, mines and quarries may be located. Stone and metals for shelter, for machinery, and for money and luxury may be dug from the bowels of the earth, by the eager imagination of the pupil. Coal and salt mines may be explained, and the wonderful story of their creation be told. We are thus brought naturally to the study of geology and mineralogy. The study of the structure, as I told you, leads directly to the study of the construction.

The earth is now made ready for the abode of man, and man, the animal, will now take his place on the earth, created in the minds of the children. Lessons should be given on the races of men; and their peculiarities, customs, and habits described. The races may be located upon the maps, by coloring the maps as the races are colored. How do men live? In what kind of houses? What clothing do they wear? What do they eat? Pupils have been prepared by the previous lessons to answer these questions, with one exception— that of the products brought from countries by commerce. Lessons on government, should now be given— how men found governments, adapted to their particular states of barbarity or civilization. Then, all the continents may be divided up by boundary lines of red chalk, into political divisions. In two or three days, if the work I have indicated has been properly done, all the political divisions of the earth, and their relative positions, may be easily taught ; and more than that, pupils will be ready to answer these questions of each political division. What is the surface and soil of this country? Climate? What the productions? The animals and race of men? The foundation thus thoroughly laid, enables the child to learn more of the world in one week, than the children who memorize the conglomerated mass of disconnected facts can learn, in a year. There is a place made for everything, and everything is put in its place.

We are now ready for the founding of cities, because we know the conditions under which cities may be founded. Here, the various industries may be grouped and studied. The farmer on his farm, the smith in his shop, the weaver at his loom. The necessity and invention of machinery, for the economizing of force. The use of steam and water power, and electricity, in manufactures. The pupils will readily discover that the countries containing small, quick-flowing rivers, must be the centres of manufacturing interests. Commerce, may be made an excellent review of what pupils have already learned. What do certain peoples want? When and how will they get it? Then comes the necessity for ships, steamers, railway cars, and beasts of burden. Routes on the ocean may be traced from city to city, and country to country, and the great lines of iron rails stretched across the continents.

The relative positions of the countries may now be fixed in the mind, by lines of latitude and longitude, and the climates may be studied on the same lines, and the causes of the differences in climate be discovered.

The next step I would suggest, is the study of a few very important countries. Important, as they relate to the world's progress and civilization. The United States should be thoroughly studied, as a preparation for our history. Great Britain, France, and Germany should be studied for the same purpose. Egypt, Palestine, Greece, Italy, and Spain, should be separately studied as a preparation for the study of Ancient History. The pupils are now ready to watch, with great eagerness and close observation, the changing mass of mankind, as they move over the stage, that has been so carefully prepared in their imagination. They are now ready for History.

Collateral reading should be kept up from the beginning to the end of all this work. Histories, adapted to the children; stories, travels, descriptions of animals and plants; all may be very profitably used at every stage of progress.

Objects—kinds of plants, woods, articles of food, clothing, fuel, implements of labor, models of shelters of all countries and nations, should be collected into a school museum, and used in teaching, as they are needed. When objects fail, pictures should be used. Of these, every teacher can easily make a very large collection, cut from illustrated papers, magazines, books, etc., neatly pasted upon cheap card-board, and classified. One set may be used for landscapes, another for water views, others for shelter, cities, animals, races of men, and the various industries.

This is but a brief outline of the new, and comparatively untried science of Geography. The great difficulty in the way of its introduction, can be traced to the terrible power of habits, fixed by our own imperfect education. The teaching of the science of Geography. depends almost entirely upon the power to use the imagination. In my limited experience, I find that the imagination, instead of being developed by the usual methods of teaching, is crushed, and nearly obliterated, so far as the action of the mind is concerned in study. The first thing for us to do, my dear teachers, is to convince ourselves, by careful and thoughtful study, that there is a real science of Geography. After this is done, we may have the courage and persistence, so much needed for its application in teaching.

TALK XXII.

HISTORY.

Two things should be acquired by the study of history in grammar schools. First, an ardent love for history; second a plan or method of studying the subject. The main practical purpose of the study of history is, to guide our steps in social, political, and religious progress. This philosophy of history, cannot be studied to any great extent until the student reaches the high school or college. The study of history in the grammar schools, should be confined to the collection and arrangement of facts necessary to the generalization upon which the philosophy of history depends. The place of history in mental development, is found in the means it affords for increasing the power of the imagination and deduction. Generalizations learned and recited by rote, before the facts are known, encumber the mind with useless rubbish. There are very few text-books that can be used profitably in grammar schools, because they are, for the most part, filled with such generalizations. Higginson's "Young Folk's History of the United States" is an exception.

The active imagination of the child, so strongly marked in his ardent love for stories, may be developed into a still greater love for history. I have spoken briefly, in a former talk, of the use of fairy and mythological stories in mental development. The child's intense desire to use his imagination continually, is the foundation of this love. Fairy stories, to the child, are like the parables of the Master; they contain the seeds of truth, that will germinate and fructify in the child's mind, far better than the truth grown to its full stature, and embodied in maxims and precepts. Every teacher should be an excellent story-teller, so as to make the half hour each day given to story-telling, a delightful one to the children. As the child gains experience, by contact and communing with his fellows, there comes a time, when the real should take the place of the fictitious, and all the child's love for fancy may be carried over and become more intensified, in his love for the real. Short, carefully selected, and well-told stories, make a good beginning for the elementary study of history. It matters not whether these stories be taken from ancient or modern history. They should be brief, simple, well told. Tell the children the story, and have them tell it back in their own language. Then let them write it, as I said in my talk upon language; this furnishes one of the best means of talking with the pencil. Work like this may be given in the fourth year. Pictures, representing historical scenes, like the "Landing of Columbus," the "Discovery of the Mississippi," etc., may be used with excellent effect, both for language and history lessons. First, have pupils describe what they see in the picture, thus arousing their curiosity, and then tell them the story. Two years, at least, may be profitably spent in this work. Reading, after the third year, of easy and interesting books upon history may be introduced. Books like "Stories of American History," Quackenbos's "Elementary History," and, Mrs. Monroe's "Our Country." These may be read as regular reading lessons. Pupils should be required to tell what they have read, both orally and in writing The sixth year may be spent to advantage in the study of the biographies of a few great men and women, around whose history very important facts can be grouped.

In the seventh year, more direct study of history should begin. It is a great mistake to teach the history of the United States, unconnected with the history of other nations, whose acts made our history possible. From 1492 on, the history of all peoples that had so much to do with the formation of our own nation ; Italy, Spain, France, Holland, Germany, and Great Britain should be studied. In teaching Spanish or French discoveries, one or more topics may be arranged for the teaching of Spain and France at the time of these discoveries. One great difficulty in the teaching of history, that puzzles teachers and text-book makers, is the immense number of facts that may be taught. A careful selection of the subjects to be taught, is of the first importance. Two rules should govern, in the selection of topics. First, select subjects that are interesting ; second, choose those topics which bear directly on the development of the progress of the nation, or upon its failure and downfall. That is, the teaching of all facts should be so directed, that the pupil when the proper time comes, may be able to study effectively the philosophy of history. The course of study in history, during the seventh and eighth years, should consist of a carefully selected and arranged number of topics, that cover the salient points in the history of a country. They should be so arranged, that one may be developed into the other, and the whole form a framework of history, into which all after facts may come in their proper places. Do not choose too many topics. One topic, so taught as to arouse genuine interest, and love for reading history, will do more good than a hundred, superficially taught. Bear in mind that your purpose is to create a love for history. You are generating a power, that is to act during the child's life. Teaching the child to memorize page after page of dry dates and empty generalizations, is the best means to induce weakness, and disgust pupils, so that they will look upon history all their days as an unpleasant study.

That which interests children the most is, the facts that come nearest to their own experience, [expanded and exaggerated, of course]. Thus, the inner life of a people may be made intensely interesting. How they lived, the kind of houses, what they ate, their clothing, customs, and manners, should form a very considerable part of all the teaching of history. Besides, in these facts, we find the true secret of the failure or growth of nations; of which the governments, wars, and great events are simply the outcome. A real picture of how a tribe or nation lives, the family and social relations, the education and customs, is of more philosophical value, than the lives of Alexander, Cæsar, or Napoleon; for the first made the latter possible, they furnished the conditions through which great men become great.

In the talks upon geography, I tried to show you of what immense importance, the knowledge of the structure of the earth's surface is, in remembering and understanding history. How the varying slopes make up the character of the continent, and influence the civilization of its peoples. The main point which I wish to impress upon you now, is, that a clear and distinct picture of the stage, upon which the drama of a nation's history moves, is absolutely essential, in fixing the various facts and scenes in the memory. The structure remains nearly the same throughout the ages, and it is only by the close association of the ever-changing scenes of time, with the clearest notions of immovable space, that these scenes can be retained in their relations and developments. The first thing to be done, then, in teaching any topic, is, to fix the stage or structure upon which the scenes were enacted, very clearly in the mind. This may be done best, by moulding the structure in sand, upon the moulding-board, and then, by drawing the horizontal outline on the blackboard. · No attempt should ever be made to teach a fact in history without the close accompaniment of moulding and drawing.

History cannot be well taught from one book. I would, if possible, have each pupil obtain a different book. There should be in every school a collection of histories for reference and reading. Works of fiction should also be included. Give out a topic, and ask pupils to read it up, mentioning the best sources of information at their disposal. In recitation, have them tell what they have read ; add to their store of knowledge by giving them your own ; arouse their curiosity, thus leading them to read in certain directions; discussions may be held on disputed points, and authorities cited. The teacher should mould all that the pupils bring, into systematic order, and, finally, when pupils are full of the subject, have them write out all they have learned. When the day of examination arrives, select one or more of the topics, and have pupils tell, with their pens, all they know about it. The marking should be upon the pupil's power of research, expression in original language, and finally upon the use of language.

Very much of the pupil's power in learning history depends upon his ability to read well, *i.e.*, to get thought accurately and rapidly by means of words. By this plan all mere rote-learning is entirely avoided. The memorizing of dates should be confined to the events that mark great epochs in history. Dates should be used simply as labels upon subjects that have been made very interesting to pupils.

The danger of using one book, is, that by it, pupils will be led to pin their faith to an author. By using many books they will soon find how facts, causes and results, differ under the different authorities. They will discover for themselves, that even the best authorities are not always reliable. The teacher should avoid dogmatic opinions in regard to politics and religion. Pupils, if left to their own research, will find out for themselves the important fact, that it was not because men were Republicans or Democrats, Protestants or Catholics, that so many bad acts have been performed by various sects and parties; but because the lust for power, and love for cruelty drives men to the commission of crime, no matter what their party name or sect may be. To teach a child that the Protestants were always right and pure, that the Catholics were always wrong and unjust, is radically false and wicked. A great love for truth and justice should be developed by real teaching. In my experience, children may be led to love the reading of history more than they do that of fiction. It is wonderful, it would seem almost incredible, if a painful experience had not taught us otherwise, that the learning of history can be made a repulsive drudgery on the part of children. Truly, the invention of the school-master has been carried to the bitter end, when children can be trained into a dislike for the study of the grand scenes of which history is so rich and full.

TALK XXIII.

EXAMINATIONS.

I believe that the greatest obstacle in the way of real teaching to-day, is the standard of examinations. The cause is not far to seek. The standard for the work has a powerful influence on the work itself. What should examinations be ? The test of real teaching—of genuine work. What is teaching ? Teaching is the evolution of thought, and thought is the mind's mode of action. Teaching arouses mental activity, so as to develop the mind in the best possible way, and at the same time, leads to the acquisition of that knowledge which is most useful to the mind and its development. There is one other important factor to be considered, and that is, the training of that skill which leads to the proper expression of the thought evolved. This factor in teaching, is usually called *training*, the results of which are correct modes of expression, such as talking, writing, drawing, making, and building. All school work, then, is comprehended in thought and its expression. It must be understood at every step, that expression is only necessary when thought is evolved. Train expression at the expense of thought, and we have the body without the living soul.

Real teaching, meaning by this the evolution of thought,

and the training of its expression, does not aim at the learning of disconnected facts. Real teaching leads to the systematic, symmetrical, all-sided upbuilding of a compact body of knowledge in the mind. Every faculty of the mind—perception, judgment, classification, reason, imagination, and memory—is brought into action in this upbuilding, or *in*struction ; and the foundations are laid broad and deep, in sense-products. Words and all other means of expression, are simply indications of thought-building, and its complicated processes. Examinations, then, should test the conditions and progress, of mind in its development. The means of examination are found in language, oral and written, in drawing, and all other forms of expression.

If I am not mistaken, the examinations usually given, simply test the pupil's power of memorizing disconnected facts. Take, for illustration, the innumerable facts in history ; of these, that which a child can learn in a course of four or five years' vigorous study would be as a drop of water to the ocean. It would be an easy matter, to set an examination of ten seemingly simple questions in history, for Mommsen, Curtius, Droysen, Bancroft, and other eminent historians, which they would utterly fail to pass. How, then, can we judge of a child's knowledge by asking ten questions ? The same can be said of geography and the natural sciences. The fact is, the only just way to examine pupils is, to find out what the teacher has taught, and her manner and method of teaching. Examination should find out what a child does know, and not what he does not know. Suppose, then, that in the example just mentioned, the pupils have been under the guidance of a skillful teacher, who has given out, one after another, the most interesting subjects to be found in history, and had her pupils read all they could find in various books about them, and after taking these acquired treasures of knowledge, and arranging the events in logical order, had finally had the children write out in good English the whole story. The test of such work would simply be, to request the pupils to tell orally, or on paper, all they knew about Columbus, Walter Raleigh, Bunker Hill, or any other interesting subject they have studied.

It is very easy, for one accustomed to such examinations, to judge of the true teaching power of the teacher by the written papers. If meaningless words have been memorized, if there is a lack of research, investigation, and original thought, the results will be painfully apparent. Whatever the teacher has done, or failed to do, can be readily comprehended by an expert in examination. In the same way geography and the sciences may be examined. The test of spelling, penmanship, composition, punctuation, and the power to use correct language, can be tested in no better way than by the writing of such compositions as these.

Examinations should not be made the test of fitness for promotion. If the teacher really teaches, and faithfully watches the mental growth of her pupils, through the work of one or two years, she alone is the best judge of the fitness of her pupils to do the work of the next grade. If she does not teach, it is impossible for her to prepare her pupils for advanced work. The great question for the supervisor to decide is, Has the teacher the ability to instruct the children in the proper manner and by the best methods? Is it possible for a supervisor to find out in one hour, by a series of set questions, more than the teacher, who watches carefully the development of her pupils for one or two years?

Those who understand children, will readily appreciate the excitement and strain under which they labor, when their fate depends upon the correct answering of ten disconnected questions. It is well known to you, that some of the best pupils, generally do their worst in the confusion that attends such highly-wrought nervous states. How much better, then, is it to take the entire work of the pupil for the whole year, than the results of one hour, under such adverse conditions?

Again, examinations demand more than the children can perform. What teacher ever received a class from a lower grade, fully prepared for the work fixed by the examination for her grade? I have never found one. Supposing children have been in the school three or four years under poor teaching, and do not know anything thoroughly—cannot read, write, reckon, or think. Now the teacher who takes such poorly prepared pupils, must choose one of two courses. She must do the children under her charge the greatest possible good, by teaching them thoroughly what they have failed to learn, and then have them fail entirely of passing the uniform examinations; or by sheer force of verbal memory, the paragraphs, pages, and propositions necessary for the test, may be put into their minds. "Having," says Spencer, "by our method induced helplessness, we straightway make helplessness the reason for our method."

Perfect freedom should be given the teacher to do the best work in her own way. That is, the highest good of the child should be the sole aim of the teacher, without the slightest regard for false standards. The teacher who strives for examinations and promotions, can never really teach. The only true motive that should govern the teacher, must spring from the truth, found in the nature of the child's mind and the subject taught.

The purpose of the superintendent's examination should be, to ascertain whether the principals under his charge, have the requisite ability and knowledge to organize, supervise, and teach a large school. The examinations of the principal, should test the teaching power of his teachers; and lastly, the teacher should test, by examinations, the mental growth of her pupils. This is the true economical system of responsibility. First, ascertain whether superintendent, principal, and teacher can be trusted, and then trust them.

The answer to this proposition, I have heard a thousand times. "Your plan would be good enough, if we had good teachers. The fault is, that the teachers are so poor we cannot trust them. If we did not examine them in this way, they would absolutely do nothing." The fallacy of this answer may be exposed in two ways. First, a uniform examination of disconnected questions, prevents the good teacher from exercising her art; second, the poor teacher will never be able to see the wide margin between good work and that which she does, until the true test of real teaching is placed before her. There has been legislation enough for poor teachers and poor teaching. Give the good teachers a chance! The testimony of countless good teachers has been uniform in this respect. When asked, "Why don't you do better work?" "Why don't you use the methods taught in normal schools, and advocated by educational periodicals and books?" The answer is, "We cannot do it. Look at our course of study. In three weeks, or months, these children will be examined. We have not one moment of time to spend in real teaching!" No wonder that teaching is a trade and not an art! No wonder there is little or no demand for books upon the science and art of teaching, such as "Payne's Lectures," etc. The demand fixed by examiners is for cram, and not for an art; and so long as the demand exists, so long will the teacher's mind shrivel and dwarf, in the everlasting treadmill that has no beginning or end, and the more it turns the more it creaks! So long, too, will this tinkering of immortal souls go on! Teachers often complain of their social position, their salaries, and the lack of sympathy in the public. "The fault," dear teachers, "is not in our stars, but in ourselves, that we are underlings." Instead of stubbornly standing, and obstinately denying that there is no need of reform, and that all so-called new methods are worthless; let us honestly, earnestly, prayerfully study the great science of teaching. Let us learn, and courageously apply the truths that shall set us free; and the day will soon come when the teacher will lead society, and mould opinion.

TALK XXIV.

SCHOOL GOVERNMENT.

The highest intellectual result brought about by elementary instruction is, the power of attention to those objects which have the greatest influence in developing the mind. It may also be said, that higher education consists in developing that power of the mind, which enables it to concentrate all its strength upon subjects within itself. To use a psychological term, the first conscious work is upon the object-object; the second, upon the subject-object. The greatest effect, either of attention or concentration, is brought about by an effort of the will, to withdraw everything from the consciousness except the object or subject of thought. The highest result of all government, from whatsoever influence it may come, is found in the most complete control of the reason over the will, in all mental and moral acts. Before the child can reason, the mother must be the child's will; but neither mother nor teacher should ever usurp the place of reason. Just as soon as a child can act from his own right impulse, he should be allowed to do so. Many a prudent parent has remained the will of the child, until the time when self-control can be acquired had past, and the moment the guidance of the parent failed, the child, often found himself drifting on the sea of life, a hopeless wreck.

The highest motive of school government, is to give the child the power and necessary reason to control himself. The immediate and direct motive of school government is, the limitation of mental power to attention. That order is the best, which leads the child to withdraw attention from all other objects except the one in hand. Whether the purpose be thinking, or performing some act of skill, or both, the direct motive of order remains the same. Attention does not consist of the attitude of the body, but of the mind. Pupils may stare intently at a book, may be paying the strictest attention, to the eyes of the teacher, while their minds are "over the hills and far away." There is a vast difference between real and apparent attention. In the one, the thing attended to, fills and controls the consciousness; in the other, the body may be in correct attitude, the eye fixed upon the object, the picture of the object may be upon the retina, but the presence of other objects of thought in the consciousness, shuts out all perception of the object seen. Attention may be impelled by a desire springing from within, from the attractiveness of the object; or compelled from without, by the will of the teacher, who expresses her will by means of rewards and punishments. The first great question, then, for the teacher to decide, is, To what extent can the attractiveness of the object be made to control attention? That is, in what measure can the interest of the child, and the love of work, be excited and quickened, so as to reduce the amount of rewards and punishments?

The natural growth of the child, both mentally and

physically, is a healthy, happy growth. That the growth may be natural, the means of growth must be exactly adapted at every step, to the varying conditions of the child. No one will deny this proposition, so far as it relates to physical growth. Food, exercise, and clothing, that meet the exact wants of the child, produce the best conditions for health and strength. I believe that this truth applies with equal power to the mind as to the body. We have many criticisms upon the so-called natural teaching, as though it were a kind of teaching, that led the child to grow in some wild, uncertain way, following his own propensities and desires. This is one of the many shallow criticisms that emanate from those who are troubled by the New Education, and not having studious habits, that would enable them to study thoroughly the reasons for better teaching, they reply to everything by stale, ready-made, stock arguments. Natural teaching, means nothing more nor less than the exact adaptation of the subject taught, to the learning mind; and that adaptation, leads the mind to grow in a normal, healthy way. As that physical exercise which is best suited to the growth and strength of the body always delights the heart, so the natural exercise of the mind must bring a still higher pleasure.

Play, is God's elementary method of training the child to work. The kindergarten is founded upon the child's intense love of play. Who ever saw anything but constant delight on the faces of the little children in a true kindergarten, where hands and heads and hearts, are in continual harmonious action? The secret lies in the fact that the child's life consists of building, weaving, drawing, taking apart and putting together, and at the same time feeding the imagination for higher flights. When should this delightful play and work stop? When the primary teacher meets him at the door of a castle, fetters his active limbs to a hard seat, and imprisons his expanding mind in a narrow cell walled by unmeaning hieroglyphics? No! A thousand times no! It is cruelty to stop the blessed work done in the kindergarten. Froebel said, that the principles he discovered and advocated, when thoroughly applied, would revolutionize the world; and he was right. In the kindergarten, is the seed-corn and germination of the New Education and the new life. The seed has been planted, the buds and flowers are turned toward the sun: let not the chilling frost of traditional teaching blight and wither them. One and all of the true principles of education are applied in the kindergarten; these principles should be applied, (simply changing the application to adapt it to different stages of growth) through all education, up to the gates of heaven.

The struggle of development, consists in acquiring knowledge and skill so thoroughly that it can sink into the automatic, thus leaving the mind free for new attainments. The conflict between the kindergarten and the old education, is the strife for the mastery, between two vastly different ideals—the ideal of quantity learning and the ideal of harmonious mental growth. The one must be compelled, as it always has been, by the rod or ignoble emulation; the other finds its glowing impulses in the inward joy of living, and growing, just as the mind's Creator designed, when He planted in the human mind, the vast possibilities to be realized by the application of His truth. I mean by this, that all the teaching in our schools, if Nature be followed, will bring decided and permanent pleasure. One great reason why we continue unnatural teaching, may be found in the fact, that the strongest tendencies and impulses of beautiful child-nature are utterly ignored. Every child loves nature : the birds, flowers, and beasts are a source of exhaustless curiosity and wonder. Carry this love into the school-room, bring the child closer and closer to the thought of God and His creatures, and that implanted desire to know more and more of His works, will never cease.

Reading, writing, spelling, numbers, are simply the means of getting an education, and they may be all beautifully taught, under the delightful stimulus of that which a child loves. The child has a strong desire to express his thoughts in the concrete, by re-creating the forms that come into his mind. He makes mud-pies, hills and valleys, fences and houses, with childish glee. Carry this same impelling tendency into the school-room ; lay the foundation of the grand science of geometry, by moulding in clay. Next to the child's love for making forms, comes the joy he finds in drawing ; a child loves to draw, as well as if not better, than he loves to talk. Continue this love, by putting crayon or pencil in his hand as soon as he enters school, and give him free room to express all he can. These tendencies are the thrifty roots of true mental and moral growth ; foster and nurture them by good teaching, and soon we will have a new and better race of men. It is a hard thing to say, but a strong belief in the immense possibilities in the human mind to grow far beyond any past attainments, compels me to express what I believe, and that is, that most primary teaching, crushes the best and highest tendencies of the mind, blights and withers imagination, stultifies reason, and then (by artificial methods) strives earnestly and honestly to build up the mind, on this ruined foundation.

I may have wandered far from my subject; but the point I wish to make, is, that the attractiveness of the subject, if naturally taught, will create a genuine enthusiastic love for study, and develop the closest and most prolonged attention, thus making the will of the teacher a secondary and subordinate element in school government. Opposed to this, is the teaching of a quantity of knowledge, and the acquisition of skill, without regard to natural adaptation. So far as my experience goes, most children are reading in books far above their range and power of thinking. They are *going through* the arithmetic, with an insufficient knowledge of the elements. They are learning page after page of generalizations and facts, that mean little or nothing to them. The teachers are preparing words for the examination, and neglecting to prepare the child for the struggle of life.

Such teaching *must*, as I have said, be enforced by the hope of rewards, or the fear of punishment. There is no alternative. The glittering bauble of a high mark, or a diploma, must lure the fainting and famished pupil on, or the rod at his back must drive him. Without these incentives there is no motion. Compare the sterility and barrenness of stupid word learning, with the richness and variety which the full action of all the mental powers—observation, judgment, imagination, and reason—causes, and we need not seek farther for the motives that induce the children, under one kind of instruction to hate school and learning; and under the other, to love school work with all their hearts.

One of the stale, old, often-repeated, stock arguments is, that the methods used, are those of entertainment and pleasure; that the child must be trained to face the stern realities of life, by strict discipline and hard work. This objection is so venerable, and at the same time so stupid, that it is hardly worth the time it takes, to answer it. Because the mind finds pleasure in natural growth, *ergo*, the teaching should be unnatural, in order to discipline its powers. As if the road to success in life, lay in tormenting the child with all the sharp thorns and hard pebbles that can be placed therein! What man ever made a true success in this world, who did not love his work, and pursue it with a genuine enthusiasm? Education is the generation of power; power to overcome obstacles, power to toil, and struggle, and fight. There are plenty of real obstacles, that lie in the pathway of human development and progress, without the invention of a single artificial one. The entire purpose of education consists of training the child to work, to work systematically, to love work, and to put his brains and heart into work. The more a child loves work, the more energy he will bring to it. The more brains he puts into it, the better, and the more economically it will be done.

I claim two things : First, that there is not one moment to spend upon anything, for the mere sake of discipline, that has not a practical use in the mind's upbuilding ; second, that if the work be adapted to the state of mental and physical power and ability ; if every onward movement brings success ; if the work be real [that is upon real things and not drudgery] ; then let the child learn to do by doing ; for the pleasure of doing and its resultant successes best fits a man to control himself, and master all the difficulties and obstacles that lie before him.

I am aware that I have been painting an ideal school, under ideal teaching. Many of you, no doubt, are anxiously asking the question, " What shall we do, who are training children who have not had the benefits of the kindergarten and the best primary teaching "? I must refer you, for the answer to this important question, to the other means of limiting attention ; *i.e.*, your wills used in governing children, who are not attracted by their work. " Fear is the beginning of wisdom." The first important element on your part, necessary to govern a school well, is self-control ; the second, courage. The children, after the innocence of the first year is past, have formed a habit that leads them to govern you, if you cannot govern them. They study you, as soldiers do a fortress that they intend to attack. If there is one weak point indicated by your presence, in movement, attitude, or expression, they will make the charge there. If you can be teased, irritated, or made angry they, will find, for want of better things, the greatest pleasure in sticking pins (figurative) into the weak places of your moral anatomy. If you threaten, they take great delight in listening to your threats. If you scold, they will invent ways of perpetuating the process. But if they see in you, a quiet, unalterable determination to control them, softened and strengthened by a great love for children, in most cases, their surrender will be complete and permanent; provided you have already at hand, some nutritious and tasteful food, in the way of good teaching and training. Give them something to do, the first moment you enter the schoolroom. Show them how skilful you are, in all points of technical training, without being ostentatious, and they will soon forget their desire to badger and control you, in the pleasure of doing.

But perfect courage and self-control are ideal again. "What if I haven't these qualities?" you ask. "How shall I meet a rebellious boy?" You see, I cannot avoid the great question of corporal punishment. Putting it in its right place, it is, at best, but a poor substitute for a teacher's lack of moral power and skill. If the choice between anarchy, misrule, and comparative order must be made, I am bound to recommend, in such cases, the judicious use of a good rattan. Corporal punishment is far preferable to scolding; that turns a schoolroom into a perpetual washing-day. It is preferable to many inventions that have been discovered to avoid straightforward punishment—such as shutting children up in dark closets, making them stand for hours in the floor, sending them home, or keeping them after school. If you punish in anger, you simply enhance the difficulty. Anger begets anger. The sting of the rod must be accompanied by the genuine sympathy of real love. This is one of the painful subjects which must be met by every teacher, until the kindergarten and true teaching, have done their effectual work with the little children. "Fear is the beginning of wisdom," but "Perfect love casteth out fear!"

TALK XXV.

MORAL TRAINING.

No matter how much educators may differ in regard to the means and methods of teaching, upon one point there is substantial agreement ; viz. that the end and aim of all education, is the development of character. There is also, little or no difference of opinion, in regard to the elements that form the common ideal of character. Love of truth, justice, and mercy ; benevolence, humility, energy, patience, and self-control, are recognized the world over, as some of the essentials that should govern human action. True character is recognized and felt, by all classes and conditions of society though they may be incapable of its analysis. Just as the lower types of intellect feel the power of the few masterpieces of art, without knowing its source.

All the knowledge and skill of an individual, all he thinks, knows, and does, is manifested in his character. Character is the summation of all these manifestations Character is the expression of all that is in the mind, and it may be analyzed into habits. A habit is the tendency and desire to do that which we have repeatedly done before. A habit then, consists in doing, the primary foundation of which, is to be found in the possibilities for action that lie latent in the mind of the new-born child. The environment of the child, determines the kind, quality, and direction of its mental action. Education adapts the environment, by limiting it to those circumstances which lead the mind to act in the right manner, and in the right direction. The mother and teacher, be it through ignorance or knowledge, determine the doing of the child. The true teacher leads the child to do that which ought to be done. The famous principle of Comenius; "Things that have to be done, should be learned by doing them," includes in its category, the whole truth that should govern every parent and teacher in building the character of a child. Everything that may determine action, be it religious precepts, moral maxims, the best influences, or whatever of good may be brought to bear upon the child, find their limitations in what they inspire, and stimulate the child to do.

The opinion prevails among many teachers, that intellectual development, is, by its nature, separate and distinct from moral training. Of all the evils in our schools, this terrible mistake is productive of the greatest. The powers of the mind determine by their limitations all human action. There is no neutral ground. Every thing done has a moral, or immoral tendency. That is, doing, forms by repetition, a habit, and habits make up character. Let no one think that I am trenching on religious or theological grounds. I simply repeat what I have said before; the greatest truths of religion, the highest forms of morality, nature and art with all their beauty, can do no more than stimulate, inspire, direct, and fix mental action. This action may be right, or wrong. If right, it leads upward to all that is good, true, and beautiful. If wrong, it leads down to falsehood, wickedness, and sin. No teacher should say, "I train the intellect," and leave moral and spiritual teaching to others. Every act of the teacher, his manner, attitude, character, all that he does, or says, all that he calls upon his pupils to do or say, develops in a degree, moral or immoral tendencies. I am aware that this is a very strong statement. I may not be able to prove it, entirely to your satisfaction, but I believe it with all my heart, and will try to give you reasons for the faith that is in me.

First, and foremost of the habits to be acquired, is that of self-control, and to self-control, we shall all agree, every act in educating the child should lead. The vices that ruin mankind, are the baneful fruitage of the lack of self-control ; and generous, humanity-loving people, spend millions to mitigate the evils arising from this lack. An ounce of prevention is worth a ton of cure ! One dollar, spent for Kindergartens, will do more in the cause of temperance, than thousands for reform schools, or Washingtonian homes. The mind is controlled by three causes. First, by the will of another. Second, by one's own desire, whether right or wrong. Third, by reason ; *i.e.*, that a course of action is knowingly right, and therefore must be taken. As I said, in the talk upon school government, the mother and teacher *must* be the will of the child, until the child's reason, or knowledge of right, leads it to do right acts. Otherwise, its own unreasoning desire will govern the will from the first. I have known many a child, tired and jaded by the care of controlling its parents, which control began, when it first cried for a light, and *got* it; and continued, up to the time that it came under the influence of the sweet strong will of a kind-hearted teacher; I have known such children, to act as though a great burden was rolled from their little shoulders, as they sat and worked, at last in perfect peace, and quietness; but alas, only to go home and resume the reins of government! The child finds true happiness alone, under the dominion of a firm, steady, reasonable will outside of himself.

But there is a dangerous and delicate point, beyond which, the will of the parent or teacher must not be carried. The moment a child can act from a dictate of his own reason, that tells him something is right, the superimposed will of the parent should give way to the child's own volition. The law, that we learn to do by doing, comes in here with full force. The importance of training the will by developing the knowledge of right, cannot be overrated. The knowledge of right, comes from leading the mind to discover the truth. The truth is of no use, unless it is expressed in action. The opportunities for this action, at home, and in school, are innumerable. These opportunities should be seized upon, and used, by the mother or teacher, as means of training self-control. I cannot repeat often enough, the great truth, that we learn to do by doing. If a child be selfish, he has acquired the habit by selfish acts. The wrong tendency may, it is true, be inborn, but the habit, is acquired by selfish doing. A bad habit can be cured, only, by repetitions of good acts, directly opposed to it. Thus, a selfish child, may be given many opportunities to perform benevolent, and generous acts. Cruelty, may be turned into loving-kindness and mercy, in the same way. In the school, we find all the primary elements of society, but lacking the conventionalities of the grown-up world ; and here, the child acts out his nature, freely. The eager, searching eye of the teacher, fixed upon the good of the child's soul, rather than the quantity of knowledge to be gained, sees through the mass of her little ones, into the weakness of each individual. The order, the writing, the reading, the number lessons, the play-ground, all furnish countless occasions, where the child may be led to act in the right way, from right motives. Selfishness may be turned to benevolence, cruelty to love, deceit to honesty, sullenness to cheerfulness, conceit to humility, and obstinacy to compliance, by the careful leading of the child's heart to the right emotion. But, in this work, the most responsible of all human undertakings, we cannot afford to experiment ; there is one indispensable requirement,—*the teacher must know the child, and its nature.*

The true method of teaching, is the exact adaptation of the subject taught, or means of growth, to the learning mind. The mind can best grow, in only one way. If the adaptation of the subject to the mind is wrong, the action of the mind is impaired, and weakened, by ineffectual attempts to grasp it ; and then the will of the teacher is obliged to come in, with artificial stimulants—to unhealthy mental action. Under such conditions, real essential happiness, that must come from the child's right emotions, is wanting ; and the subject becomes in itself, an object of dislike and disgust to the child. Such teaching, I hold, must be, of its very nature, immoral. On the other hand, when the mind is in the full tide of healthy normal action, when it loves what it does, and does what it loves, the leading power of the teacher, in right directions, is enhanced to an incalculable degree. If the teacher knows the child, and her heart lies close to the child's heart, every motion of his mental and moral pulse, every desire to do wrong, or right, will always be felt by her. However much the teacher may desire to help the child, however strong her own moral or religious feelings may be, wrong methods, and misapplied teaching, stand as formidable barriers between herself and the child. Many a father who would have given his life for his boy, has, simply because he did not understand his child's nature, failed in his method of training, and driven the boy to ruin. The will of a parent, may deprive the child of the use of his reason so long, that when the controlling will is removed, the child finds himself weak, and helpless; a prey to any stronger will that may chose to master him.

Primary education consists, as I have said, in training the power of attention. The attractiveness of the object attended to, controls the will. The desire to attend, is thus aroused, making it possible for the mind to exert more and more power in such acts, until the reason comes in to govern the will, enabling the mind to concentrate itself whenever required. The boy who is trained to solve a difficult problem, by a long and labored struggle with the thought, stimulated only by the desire that comes from former successes to gain a new victory, has a will trained by reason in a high degree. You may say that this boy, notwithstanding his power in one direction, might perform immoral acts; and you are right. The energy generated in one direction, if it be not broadened and deepened in all other right ways, may be fatal to the welfare of the possessor. Lead and train a child to do one good thing thoroughly, through love of doing, and you have a central force of moral power, that can be turned into all doing.

Let us look for a moment on the other side of this question. God has so created the mind, that healthy moral, mental, and physical exercise, produces pleasure; this truth, I believe, cannot be gainsaid. If the work be not adapted to the grasp of the pupil, this pleasurable stimulant is lacking, and artificial stimulants must be used. I have discussed, in a former talk, the use of fear in governing children. I need but appeal to all those, into whose heads knowledge has been driven by the terror of punishment, to obtain the strongest testimony, that such a course invariably disgusts children with learning, and defeats the ends it seeks to promote. The ubiquitous croaker now arises, with his single, ever reiterated poser: "Webster, Clay, Sumner, and all our greatest, were educated in the old ways, why require better methods when we can point to such results as these?" My dear sir; you can count, it is true, a few saved and successful men and women, but is your power of calculation great enough, to count the failures, the lost? It is time for us, teachers, to call a halt! All about us are men and women, who find themselves, to-day, crippled, for want of that power which their school-training should have given them. You feel the same lack, and so do I. Now, these men and women, have risen up, and are demanding better things for their children. We have but to look, to see the hand-writing on the wall,—" Thou art weighed in the balances, and art found wanting."

The other artificial stimulant, is the hope of reward, in the shape of merits, per cents, prizes ;—glittering empty baubles ; sugar-coated but bitter pills ! I have not time to point out, in detail, the immoral influences of these false stimulants. I will allude to one, and that is, the common tendency in examinations to appropriate other's earnings. How common this is, you all know, from primary school to college. Ponies, cuffs, hidden slips of paper, sly glances at books, promptings, and the thousand and one means to present stolen results ; all testify to the prevalence of this evil. This is nothing more nor less than systematic training in habits of dishonesty. I have no doubt, that many of the frauds and defalcations, so common at present in this country, may be traced directly back to the well-meant, but dishonest training in the school-room.

Truth should govern the will, and the great work of the teacher is, to guide the child in his discoveries of truth. The habit of searching, finding, and using the truth, then, is one of the first importance. Truth sets the child free, and leads him to the source of all truth. The highest freedom is obedience to God. The learning of words, and pages of the text-books, without the privilege of verifying the facts and generalizations there given, weakens the reasoning power, that should be developed for the purpose of controlling the will. I do not here refer to religious truths, but to the habit of seeking and prizing the truth, wherever found in the branches taught in our common schools. If this habit is formed there, it will be carried into the affairs of politics, and society. For instance; a man so trained, will vote, not because he happens to belong to a party, or because he believes the *ipse dixit* of a leader; but because, through force of habit, he will discover from all the sources of information that lie in his power, what the truth really is, and exercise his right to vote accordingly. "Put that you would have the State, into the school," is an old German maxim. Americans must learn to apply this saying in a vigorous way, or our politics, from their downward tendency, will reach in no far distant day, their lowest level.

There are two factors in education;—thought, and expression. Most teaching, is the training of the skill to express thought, with little or no regard to the thought itself. Precision, is an indispensable mode of training skill in writing, drawing, position, and accurate ways of acting; but, when the training of precision is made the main motive of school-work; when the ways a child sits, places his feet, holds his hands, stares at a book, stands up, marches, utters a sentence, etc. are the be all and end all in the teacher's plan of work; then, precision invades the sacred realm of thought evolution, and the mind's power to act is crushed and crippled. I have seen schools of this description where the results would be grand, if the systematic clock-work-like operations were performed with puppets, instead of living human beings. Such training educates the willing followers of demagogues; prompt to march when the commanding boss gives the word.

Conceit is another outgrowth of this quantity ideal. The spectacle is a common one, of a young man, the model of his class, persistent and alert, possessed of a powerful verbal memory, which enables him to cram page after page of the text-book, distancing all competitors, carrying off all the class honors, and finally; armed with his sheepskin, [his Alma Mater's gracious indorsement of his wonderful attainments] confidently stepping out into the world, never questioning but that he will conquer in the new life, as easily as he did in the old. But the first spear-thrust of reality shivers his panoply of empty words, and leaves him defenceless, before the rigorous demands of an uncompromising world. "The long perspective of our life is truth, and not a show;" and I hold that sort of teaching, in the highest degree immoral, which crams the heads of our children, with the unusable pages of text-books, and then leads them to suppose that they are gaining real knowledge. By making quantity our ideal, we develop and foster conceit; and conceit is one of the most formidable barriers to true knowledge.

Inspire them to seek earnestly for the truth, and develop in them, one of the greatest of all human virtues—humility. "The meek shall inherit the earth," said the Great Teacher. He alone is really learning, who feels the immensity of the truth, and realizes that all he knows, or can know, in this world, is but as a drop to the great ocean of truth, that stretches boundless and fathomless into eternity. The teacher, above all others, should constantly be adding to his store of knowledge; and he who imagines that he has no more to learn in the art of teaching, is fit only to take his small place among other fossils.

Primary education consists, as I have repeatedly tried to show, in the development of the power of attention; and it will be plain to all, that the selection of the objects of thought and attention is a matter of the highest importance. The things presented must be pure, good, and beautiful, for that to which we attend, comes into the heart, and forms the basis of all our thinking and imagination; "Out of the heart the mouth speaketh." Where shall we look for the highest source of the good, the true, and the beautiful? To the thoughts of God in nature. The study of nature, is the best and highest foundation for morality, and a preparation for the revealed truth, that comes to the child later in life. Compare the drill upon hieroglyphics, empty words, and meaningless forms, with the observation of trees, flowers, animals, and the forms of earth. The one stimulates thought, and fills the mind with ideas of beauty; the other crowds the mind with useless, ugly forms that cannot, from their very nature, stimulate it to renewed action. A child's mind, filled with that which is pure, and good, has no room for wickedness and sin. The study of the natural sciences, is one of the best means of bringing about this result. Did you ever observe the character of a boy who early fell in love with nature, and who spent his spare hours with plants, or animals, seeking for their haunts, watching their habits, and making collections for preservation? Such boys, so far as I have known, are genuinely good. They have neither the time, nor the inclination, for evil doing. The study of the thoughts of God in nature, filling the mind, as it does, with things of beauty, prepares the imagination for clear and strong conceptions of the higher and spiritual life.

Let no one misunderstand me, or imagine for a moment, that I mean to limit moral training to these subjects. Far from it. I am only trying to show, how all these things may be used in developing true character. Children learn very much by imitation. The teacher, whether good or bad, leaves his everlasting imprint on every child under his care. He can conceal nothing from the intuitional power of the child. Whatever you are, becomes immortal through the souls of your pupils. The precepts of a true teacher have immense weight; but the example has a still greater.

A fact very much bemoaned and bewailed in these times, is, that children love to read trashy literature; that they read Dime Novels, sensational newspapers, and stories like, The Robber of the Bloody Gulch or The Red Handed Pirate of the Spanish Main. This unwholesome, and vicious tendency, is almost wholly caused, I believe, by the neglect of school authorities to furnish a generous supply of pure, interesting literature, to the schools under their charge. I know a superintendent of schools who often waxes eloquent over the vices engendered by such reading. I once visited his schools, and found his pupils learning to spell column after column, and page after page of words, one-tenth of which, they probably never would use in their lives. I satisfied myself that these poor victims hardly knew the meaning of one word, the forms of which they were struggling over. The money expended for those spelling-books, would have purchased a rich supply of excellent reading; and the time thrown away in conning that fearful book, if used in reading the best literature, would have rendered unnecessary some of that superintendent's eloquent, and pathetic periods, in regard to the miseries caused by reading sensational works. An entire year of the little child's life is generally given to the reading of one book, not much thicker than my little finger. Let a child read a selection twice or three times, and he knows every word by heart. He can after that read his lesson with the book upside down. I once tested one of the best schools in this country. The pupils read very well indeed, I asked them to close their books; and as soon as they understood what I wanted, they repeated every word, verbatim, with great gusto, simply by my reading one word, anywhere in the book. They knew that book from beginning to end; and yet, following the course of study, they must repeat those words, over and over again, for five long months! We are paying millions of dollars, in this country, for such worse than stupid and useless repetitions. A class will read a Primary Reader through in a very short time. The cost of a dozen different series of books [bought by the school authorities] is not so great as the price paid, by the children, for the Readers of a single series. Every school can, and should have a good library, made of sets of different books, embracing ; the best Readers ; works on natural history adapted to children, such as, Prang's little books, "Little Folks in Feathers and Fur," "Life and Her Children," and "The Fairyland of Science ;" primary geographies, like "Our World," and Guyot's "Introduction ;" histories ; books of travel ; poetry ; and the best fiction. In my experience, it is the easiest of all problems, to lead children to read, and to love to read, the very best literature. If the hours devoted to the spelling-book ; to useless repetitions of words already learned ; were spent in the perusal of the best books, children would never feel the necessity for the trash they read, whose baneful influence is immeasurable.

In my talk upon School Government, I said, that the end and aim of school education, is to train a child to work, to work systematically, to love work, and to put his brains into work. The clearest expression of thought, is expression in the concrete. Working with the hands, is one great means of primary development. It is also one of the very best means of moral training. From the first, every child has an intense desire to express his thought in some other way, than in language. Froebel discovered this, and founded the Kindergarten. No one can deny, that true Kindergarten training is moral training. Ideas and thoughts come into the mind, demanding expression. The use of that which is expressed, to the child, is the means it gives him, to compare his thought, with its concrete expression. The expression of the form made, compared with the ideal, stimulates to further trials. In making and building, is found the best means of training attention.

I wish to make a sharp distinction here, between *real work*, and *drudgery*. Real work is done on real things, producing tangible results, results that are seen and felt. Real work is adapted at every step to the child's power to do. Every struggle brings success, and makes better work possible. Drudgery, on the other hand, is the forced action of the mind upon that which is beyond mental grasp, upon words that cannot be apprehended, upon lessons not understood. Drudgery, consists, mainly, of the monotonous use of the verbal memory. There is no variety; not a bush or shrub along the pathway. This is the kind of study that produces ill-health. It is the straining of the mind upon disliked subjects, with the single motive, to gain applause, rewards, and diplomas. Thousands of nervous, earnest, faithful girls, spurred on by unwise parents, yearly lose their lives, or become hopeless invalids, in this costly and useless struggle. Real work stimulates every activity of mind and body. It furnishes the variety so necessary to interest, and is like true physical development that exercises every muscle and strengthens the whole man. Real work is always interesting, like real play. No matter how earnest the striving may be, it is followed by a glow of genuine pleasurable emotion.

There is great outcry against our schools and colleges, caused by the suspicion that they educate children to be above manual labor. This suspicion is founded upon fact, I am sorry to say; but the statement of the fact is not correct. Children are educated *below* manual labor.

The vague, meaningless things they learn, are not adapted to real work ; no effectual habits of labor are formed by rote-learning. The student's desire is too often, when he leaves school or college, to get a living by means of empty words. The world has little or no use for such rubbish. That man should gain his bread by the sweat of his brow, is a curse changed to the highest possible blessing. The clergyman, the lawyer, the physician, the teacher, need the benefit of an early training in manual labor, quite as much as the man who is to labor with his hands all his life. Manual labor is the foundation of clear thinking, sound imagination, and good health. There should be no real difference between the methods of our common schools, and the methods of training in manual labor schools. A great mistake has been made in separating them. All school work should be real work. We learn to do by doing. "Satan finds some mischief still, for idle hands to do." The direct influence of real work is, to absorb the attention in the things to be done ; leaving no room in the consciousness for idleness, and its consequent vices. Out of real work, the child develops a motive, that directs his life work. Doing work thoroughly, has a great moral influence. One piece of work well done, one subject well mastered, makes the mind far stronger and better, than a smattering of all the branches taught in our schools. School work, and manual labor, have been for a long time divorced ; I predict that the time is fast coming, when they will be joined in indissoluble bonds. The time too, is coming, when ministers will urge upon their hearers, the great importance of manual labor, as a means of spiritual growth. At no distant date, industrial rooms will become an indispensable part of every good school; the work of the head, and skill of the hand, will be joined in class-room, and workshop, into one comprehensive method of developing harmoniously the powers of body, mind, and soul. If you would develop morality in the child, train him to work.

In all that I have said, and whatever mistakes I have made, either in thought or expression, I have had but one motive in my heart, and that is, that the dear children of our common country, may receive at our hands, a development of intellectual, moral, and spiritual power, that will enable them to fight life's battle, to be thoughtful conscientious citizens, and prepare them for all that may come thereafter. Whatever we would have our pupils, we must be ourselves.

www.ingramcontent.com/pod-product-compliance
Lightning Source LLC
Chambersburg PA
CBHW020244170426
43202CB00008B/216